MILLER'S ANTIQUES CHECKLIST: FURNITURE

Consultant: Richard Davidson

First published in Great Britain in 1991 by Miller's
an imprint of Reed Consumer Books Limited
Michelin House,
81 Fulham Road
London SW3 6RB
and Auckland, Melbourne, Singapore and Toronto

Series Editor	Francis Gertler
Series Art Editor	Nigel O'Gorman
Art Editor	Christopher Howson
Illustrators	Karen Cochrane
	John Hutchinson
Editorial Assistants	Katie Martin-Doyle
	Jaspal Bhangra
Design Assistant	Elaine Hewson
Typesetter	Kerri Hinchon
Production	Barbara Hind
	Ted Timberlake

© 1991 Reed International Books Limited
Reprinted 1994

A CIP catalogue record for this book is available
from the British Library

ISBN 0 85533 88 9 X

Text film by Mitchell Beazley
Reproduction and camera work by Scantrans Plc., Ltd, Singapore
Printed and bound in China
Produced by Mandarin Offset

CONTENTS

TABLES

DINING FURNITURE

WRITING FURNITURE

BOOKCASES AND CABINETS

MISCELLANEOUS

INTRODUCTION

Antique furniture has for many years proven to be a very good investment and English furniture in particular has risen in price over the last twenty years, perhaps more than any other form of investment. Although the price of much antique furniture has risen beyond the means of many people, there are still areas that are undervalued and where there is good investment potential without substantial capital outlay. However, for most private buyers the primary reason for buying furniture is always a genuine liking for the piece. The better informed you are about the main buying factors – style, materials and methods of construction – the more likely you are to make a wise purchase, and the more you will enjoy the experience of looking at and buying antique furniture.

Antique furniture varies considerably in style depending mainly on the period and country in which it was made. Most collectors tend to be attracted to only one area of this wide field – for example, to the exuberance of Victorian furniture, or perhaps the relative simplicity of some earlier furniture.

For the private buyer there are two main sources of supply: antiques stores and auction houses. Don't be afraid to ask questions – a good dealer or auctioneer will be happy to give advice about buying and maintaining furniture. Always obtain an invoice with a description of the piece, together with an indication of its date. At auction houses, read the catalogue description carefully as this will form the basis of the purchase invoice.

It is essential when buying furniture to be able to distinguish between a "right" and "wrong" piece. There are many fakes and reproductions around, as well as pieces that were simply "updated" to make them more fashionable. A methodical approach to examining furniture will help the collector to detect a wrong piece and to assess whether any restoration has been skilfully carried out and is acceptable or not. However, as well as looking at details, it is always a good idea to stand back and gain an overall impression of a piece: fakers usually slip up somewhere and anyone familiar with the general profile of a right piece will in time be able to recognize furniture that has been tampered with or faked. The collector will gain a wealth of information from this book, but nothing can replace direct experience: the more familiar you are with the genuine article, whether from examining it, for example in a museum or stately home, the better able you will be to make an informed purchase.

The *Furniture Checklist* provides the beginner and experienced collector alike with hundreds of helpful hints and tips, and a method of assessing any piece of furniture that will help demystify an apparently complex subject and initiate you into the joys of collecting antique furniture.

RICHARD DAVIDSON

HOW TO USE THIS BOOK

When I first started collecting antiques although there were many informative books on the subject I still felt hesitant when it came to actually buying an antique. What I really wanted to do was interrogate the piece – to find out what it was and whether it was genuine.

The *Furniture* Checklist will show you how to assess a piece as an expert would, and provides checklists of questions you should ask before making a purchase. The answer to most (if not all) of the questions should be "yes", but remember there are always exceptions to the rule: if in doubt, seek expert guidance.

The book is divided into categories of furniture. At the front of the book is a section on the principal woods and how to identify them, and on factors common to all types of furniture – for example, methods of construction, patina, decoration, condition and restoration. At the back of the book is a glossary, a list of main makers and a bibliography.

Treat the book as a knowledgeable companion, and soon you will find that antique collecting is a matter of experience, and of knowing how to ask the right questions.

JUDITH MILLER

Each double-page spread looks at items belonging to a particular category of collecting.

The first page shows a carefully-chosen representative item of a type that can usually be found at antiques stores or auction houses (rather than only in museums).

The caption gives the date and dimensions of the piece shown, and a code for the price range of this type of article.

A checklist of questions gives you the key to recognizing, dating and authenticating antique pieces of the type shown.

TRIPOD TAB

An English Chippendale-period mahogany c.1755, ht 27¹/₄in/70.5cm, dia 29¹/₄in/74cm,

Identification checklist for 18thC tri
1. Is the table mahogany?
2. Is it made in the solid?
3. Do the top and bottom belong toge
4. Is there any carved decoration?
5. Does the table rest on a baluster c
Alternatives are reeded, leaf-carved c
6. Are the legs and top well-proportio
spread to the base?
7. Does the table top either tilt or ro

Variations
* Country-made tripod tables are found in oak, fruitwoods and elm.
* Although the tops of the best tripod tables are made from one piece of timber, in many perfectly good examples they are made up

of three p
Americal
Tripod tal
American
were ofte
and cherr

96

Useful background information is provided about the craftsman, factory or type of ware.

The second page shows you what details to look for.

Tripod tables
The tripod table was introduced in England during the 1730s, and was most popular in the Chippendale period. Most are found in the solid, although some small occasional tripod tables of the late 18thC are veneered. Tops are usually round, although square and oval examples are found.

Feet
The separate sole underneath the foot is a sign of quality. The casters are original and retain the original leather around the wheel (a feature found on small casters of the 18thC).

Information helps you to detect fakes, copies and reproductions.

The tilt-top mechanism
Except in the smallest tripods, the tops are made so that they can tilt to a vertical position allowing the table to be stored in a corner of the room when not in use. Typically, the base of the table tenons into a block at the top of the column. The top is fixed by means of two bearers and held in place with a brass catch. There should be signs on the underside of the top where it has rested on the block.

Bird-cage mechanism
Many tilt top tables of the period have a "bird-cage" support, as in the example above. The bird-cage is fixed to the underside of the table top and the whole mechanism slots into the top of the pedestal. A peg through the stem allows the top to rotate, tilt, or be fixed in place. (The marks around the edge of the top were made by a sewing instrument that was once attached to the table.)

Further photographs show:
* items in a similar style by the same craftsman or factory
* similar, but perhaps less valuable wares that may be mistaken for the more collectable type
* common variations on the piece shown in the main picture
* similar wares by other craftsmen
* the range of shapes or decorative motifs associated with a particular factory or period.

Dished tops
Many tripod table tops have been dished, or hollowed out, from a plain top at a later date to increase the value of the table. As tripod-table tops are relatively shallow, the screws that attach the bearers to the top sit just below the surface. If a top has been dished out, its thickness will be reduced and the screw-holes will show through. However skilfully these holes are plugged, they cannot be disguised against close inspection.
97

Construction
The cabriole legs of tripod tables are made individually and dovetailed into the central column (above). They may be strengthened from underneath with a wrought-iron bracket.

Marks, signatures and serial numbers are explained.

Hints and tips help you to assess factors that affect value – for example, condition and availability.

The codes are as follows:

A £20,000+ ($30,000+)
B £15-20,000 ($22,500-30,000)
C £10-15,000 ($15-22,500)
D £5-10,000 ($7,500-15,000)

E £2-5,000 ($3-7,500)
F £1-2,000 ($1,500-3,000)
G £500-1,000 ($750-1,500)
H under £500 ($750)

PERIODS AND STYLES

Dates	British Monarch	British Period	French Period
1558-1603	Elizabeth I	Elizabethan	Renaissance
1603-1625	James I	Jacobean	
1625-1649	Charles I	Carolean	Louis XIII (1610-43)
1649-1660	Commonwealth	Cromwellian	Louis XIV (1643-1715)
1660-1685	Charles II	Restoration	
1685-1688	James II	Restoration	
1688-1694	William & Mary	William & Mary	
1694-1702	William III	William III	
1702-1714	Anne	Queen Anne	
1714-1727	George I	Early Georgian	Régence (1715-23)
1727-1760	George II	Early Georgian	Louis XV (1723-74)
1760-1811	George III	Late Georgian	Louis XVI (1774-93) Directoire (1793-99) Empire (1799-1815)
1812-1820	George III	Regency	Restauration (1815-30)
1820-1830	George IV	Regency	
1830-1837	William IV	William IV	Louis Philippe (1830-48)
1837-1901	Victoria	Victorian	2nd Empire (1848-70) 3rd Republic (1871-1940)
1901-1910	Edward VII	Edwardian	

German Period	U.S. Period	Style	Principal woods
Renaissance (to c.1650)	Early Colonial	Gothic	Oak period (to c.1670)
		Baroque (c.1620-1700)	
Renaissance/ Baroque (c.1650-1700)			Walnut period (c.1670-1735)
	William & Mary		
	Dutch Colonial	Rococo (c.1695-1760)	
Baroque (c.1700-30)	Queen Anne		
Rococo (c.1730-60)	Chippendale (from 1750)		Early mahogany period (c.1735-70)
Neo-classicism (c.1760-1800)		Neo-classical (c.1755-1805)	Late mahogany period (c.1770-1850
	Early Federal (1790-1810)		
Empire (c.1800-15)	American Directoire (1798-1804)	Empire (c.1799-1815)	
	American Empire (1804-15)		
Biedermeier (c.1815-48)	Later Federal (1810-30)	Regency (c.1812-30)	
Revivale (c.1830-80)		Eclectic (c.1830-80)	
	Victorian		
Jugendstil (c.1880-1920)		Arts & Crafts (c.1880-1900)	
	Art Nouveau (c.1900-20)	Art Nouveau (c.1900-20)	

WOODS

Early furniture was made from solid timber planed to the desired thickness. As furniture-making techniques and styles developed it was sometimes found advantageous to apply *veneers* – thin sheets of wood, usually richly figured – over a solid surface. The veneers used on antique furniture are hand-cut and relatively thick (approx. 0.03-0.06in/1-2mm) and uneven (unlike modern veneers, which are uniform and very thin). The thickness of any veneers can be inspected at the edges – for example, of cupboard doors, where they are laid onto the framework, and at the back of a chest where the veneer is laid onto the top.

Veneering is not only economic. When cut diagonally across a log it produces a highly figured effect not usually found when planked. The most desirable veneers are burrs, taken from the most tightly knotted parts of the tree. Some timbers, such as satinwood, kingwood and coromandel, are used generally only in veneer form. This is usually because of the scarcity, and consequently the price, of the wood or because the small size of the timber does not make it suitable for constructional purposes. Other timbers, primarily mahogany and walnut, are used equally successfully in the solid and in veneer form. There are also timbers used mainly in the solid, such as oak, elm, chestnut and cherry. These are associated with country furniture.

Timber that is used for drawer linings, the carcass of the piece and the back, is known as *secondary wood*. In England this is primarily oak and pine but a variety of other woods are used. In a high-fashion piece mahogany may be used as the secondary wood. Some furniture is partially veneered and partially in the solid.

The principal woods

There is no easy way to learn to distinguish between the many types of wood – there is no substitute for first-hand experience. However, some historical background is also essential: you need to know the principal woods and the periods when they were in use. The main woods you are likely to encounter are listed below.

Amboyna

A richly coloured wood with a tight grain, similar to burr walnut, used during the 18thC and Regency periods, nearly always as a veneer.

Beech

A brownish-white wood used in the solid from the 17thC for the frames of upholstered furniture, as it does not split when tacked. It was also the base for much painted and gilded furniture.

Cherry

An orange-brown colour when polished, this wood was used in the solid for much American Queen Anne and Chippendale furniture.

Chestnut

This ranges in tone from light to dark brown. It was used extensively in the 18thC for French provincial furniture, mainly in the solid.

Coromandel

A dark, boldly figured wood, almost black in parts, with pale streaky areas; mostly used as a veneer for some high-fashion furniture of the late 18thC and Regency periods.

Ebony

A dense and heavy wood which is almost black when polished.

Elm

A light brown hardwood used prinicpally in the solid for Windsor chairs and other English provincial furniture.

Kingwood and tulipwood

Similar woods from the West Indies of orange/brown colour and with a striped figuring, used by French cabinet-makers during the 18thC as a veneer for fine furniture. Kingwood and tulipwood were used to a lesser extent in England during the last quarter of the 18thC but extensively for bandings.

Mahogany

There are several types of mahogany of which San Domingan, Cuban, Honduras and Spanish are the most important. Mahogany was imported into England from the Americas from c.1730 when it became very popular with cabinet-makers, and has been used ever since. Quality varies: at best this wood has a

beautiful rich golden colour, but it can look bland if of poor quality. The Victorians tended to polish it to a red colour. The natural finish is preferred today. Mahogany was used extensively in England and the United States in both the solid (*above top*) and as a veneer (*above bottom*).

Oak
Hard and coarse-grained, oak was the predominant wood in Britain from the Middle Ages until the late 17thC; it was used extensively in the United States and to a lesser extent in Europe. Oak was also employed as a secondary wood on quality furniture.

Olive
A hard green-yellow wood used principally in England in the late 17thC in veneer form in parquetry and oysterwork (see p.15) and for applied mouldings.

Pine
A soft, pale wood used in England and the United States as a secondary timber for drawer linings, backboards and so on, and in the production of cheap furniture during the 19thC, when it was often painted.

Rosewood
A highly figured dark wood with almost black streaks, used predominantly during the Regency period in England,

mainly as a veneer. Over time it can fade to quite a pale colour.

Satinwood
The West Indian variety is a beautiful yellow colour and was much favoured by cabinet-makers in England during the late 18thC. It was not often used in the solid, as it was very expensive.

Tulipwood See **Kingwood and tulipwood**

Virginia walnut
This rich American walnut resembles mahogany when polished. It was used in solid and veneered form on English and American furniture from c.1730.

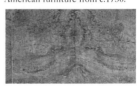

Walnut
A highly figured wood sometimes of nutty brown colour, used in England in the solid on fashionable furniture from 1660 until c.1690. From c.1690 until c.1735 walnut-veneered furniture was predominant in England. Walnut was also used extensively in the United States and Europe and became very popular in the Victorian era.

Yew
A red-brown hardwood that is found in either veneered or solid form on much of the very best English provincial furniture of the 17th and 18thC.

11

BASICS (1)

There are certain basic factors common to most pieces of antique furniture that should be part of any assessment carried out before making a purchase, in order to determine whether the piece is original, desirable, and worth the asking price. The following six pages discuss these basic points, which apply to most or all of the pieces shown in this book.

COLOUR AND PATINA

Colour is important: the timber used may or may not be a naturally good colour, while other pieces develop a fine colour over the years with the cumulative effects of sunlight and waxing. Patina is the natural build-up of wax polish and dirt that gives antique furniture a rich, soft look, which develops over many years and is not easy to fake. Assessing the colour and patina is largely a matter of first-hand experience – examine and handle as much antique furniture as possible. A knowledge of different timbers is also important (see pp.10-11).

METHOD AND QUALITY OF CONSTRUCTION

The *joined style of construction*, using mortice-and-tenon joints, held by pegs or dowels rather than glue or screws, was common until the late 17thC. Hand-made pegs are irregular in shape, and being tapered, pulled the joint tight as they were knocked in. Thus they stand slightly proud of the surface and as a result, have developed a higher polish. Later replacements, using machine-made dowelling, are perfectly circular and either flush with the surface or slightly recessed. Hand-made nails with large irregular heads were also used in the construction of early furniture, often in place of dovetailing of drawers, and on provincial furniture the use of nails continued through the 18thC.

From the Queen Anne period (1702-14) construction was more sophisticated, with greater use of dovetailing (see right) and glued joints. Until the end of the 18thC the wood for carcasses was sawn by hand, which resulted in straight saw marks. From the end of the 18thC the circular saw was used. This leaves circular marks on the surface of the wood.

In the early 19thC the introduction of mass-production

led to a general decline in quality, although the finest Victorian pieces are better made than those of any other period.

Screws

The earlier the screw the cruder it will be. The groove on top of old screws tends to be off-centre and the top irregular. The thread is also irregular and open, and often runs the length of the shank. The groove on a modern screw is perfect, of uniform shape and centred. The shank of a modern screw is part thread and part plain and terminates in a perfect point.

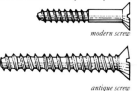

modern screw

antique screw

FEET

Styles of feet are one of the most useful guides to dating (see pp. 110-13). However, many feet were replaced when they became worn, or as fashions changed. Close inspection under the piece may be necessary to determine whether the current feet are original or not. The two most usual types are bun feet and bracket feet.

DRAWERS

Each drawer should be thoroughly inspected to ensure that there are no (or very few) replacement parts and that each matches the other. The more replacements, the lower the value of the piece.

The *dovetails* are the joints at the corners of the drawers where the pieces have been slotted together (see p. 25). These were relatively large and crude in the 17thC, but became progressively finer throughout the 18th and 19thC and thus are a good aid to dating.

Until the 18thC drawers had channels in their sides which ran on *runners* set into the carcass. From the Queen Anne period the runners were placed underneath the drawer, at the sides, and ran on bearers placed along the inside of the carcass. Runners are particularly prone to wear: replacements are acceptable.

Drawer linings are oak or pine, and on some finer pieces of the 18thC, mahogany. In the 17thC they were chunky (approx.

³/₄in/2cm thick) in order to accommodate the channels in the drawer sides. However, in the 18th and 19thC, when drawer runners were placed underneath the drawers, the linings became finer – around ¹/₄in (0.5cm) thick.

Early drawer bottoms frequently have a gap between the boards, caused by *shrinkage*. A sliver of wood can be inserted, or the underside of the drawer can be taped with a strip of fine hessian soaked in glue.

Inside, most drawers will be left unpolished (apart from some 19thC and Edwardian drawers, which are lightly polished) and should have a dry undisturbed look.

Drawer fronts
In the 17thC drawer fronts are moulded, or have simple, raised decoration, often of geometric form. The edges of the drawers are plain, although the drawer dividers have applied decorative mouldings. From the 18thC drawer fronts are flat, and finished off with overlapping ovolo (quarter-round) moulding or, from c.1725, a beaded moulding known as cock beading. The drawer dividers are plain.

HANDLES
Like feet, these are an important aid to dating as they vary from period to period (see pp. 26-7). However, they should not be used as the sole guide to dating as they may be later replacements – handles were often changed to re-fashion a piece – for example, a Queen Anne item may have Chippendale handles.

Until the late 17thC handles are held in place with a brass or iron split pin, which is pushed through the drawer, then split open to secure the handle. From c.1690 handles are usually held by pommels and nuts.

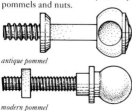

antique pommel

modern pommel

Antique pommels are hand-cast in one piece in brass. The thread goes only halfway up the shank

and the remainder of the shank is square-section (which holds better in the locating hole). A feature of these pommels is that the heads are often nicely detailed. The head of a modern pommel will be made of brass and the shank in steel, with the thread running the length of the shank. There is no squared section at the top. The brass is whiter than antique brass (as there is a lower percentage of copper in the brass alloy). The heads are usually relatively coarse.

The nuts used to secure handles in the 18thC are circular and irregular in shape, whereas modern nuts are regular and hexagonal.

Handles that have been on a piece for a long time will have built up a layer of dirt and grease on the front of the drawer, causing dark shading around the edges and in the crevices. There may also be marks where the moving parts of the handles have swung and knocked against the wood over the years.

Replacement handles
The drawer front may show the outline of other handles, or scars where the wood has been damaged in changing the handles. If the current handles are replacements there will probably be plugged holes behind the drawer fronts in the handle area where the earlier ones were fixed – possibly as many as five or six sets. Furniture that retains the original handles usually commands a premium. However, such pieces are increasingly difficult to find and replacements are generally regarded as acceptable provided that there are no bad scars on the drawer fronts and that the handles are stylistically correct for the period and are of good quality.

LOCKS
Locks on early furniture are usually of wrought iron and are held in place with hand-made iron nails. From the 18thC locks were steel or brass and secured with steel screws, the heads of brass screws being too soft. Locks from the 19thC are of brass. It is not serious if a lock has been replaced, although it is preferable to have the original one. Filled-in spaces around the present lock indicate that the original lock has been replaced.

BASICS (2)

ESCUTCHEONS

There are two types of escutcheon: one an inset brass keyhole, and the other an applied plate around the keyhole, which may reflect the style of handles used. Escutcheons are a good aid to dating and to the country of origin. Continental keyhole escutcheons are larger and more angular than those of English and American furniture. English and American escutcheons are rounded at the bottom until c.1870, after which time they have squared bottoms.

CARVED DECORATION

Carving was popular on furniture from all periods (although oak is not easy to carve). On early furniture the carving is relatively restrained compared to some of the more intricate pieces from the 18thC, especially the Chippendale period. It is important to learn how to distinguish between original carved decoration and that which has been done at a later date to "improve" a piece in appearance and value. A piece that is later carved will be worth much less than an item with original carving. This knowledge can really only be gained with experience developed from observing pieces known to be genuine.

Most 17th and 18thC furniture is carved from the solid rather than applied. Carving from the 17thC and earlier will have developed a well-patinated and soft appearance, while that from the 18thC at its best will be crisp, with undercutting (carved at an angle). Although carving from the Victorian period is often highly competent, much of it is somewhat crude and stiff by comparison, and lacks the patinated edges and natural build-up of dirt and wax in the crevices that is characteristic of 17th and 18thC carved pieces.

Applied carving is a comparatively inexpensive method employed by some 19th and 20thC reproduction firms.

VENEERS

Veneering (see p. 10) was first used during the second half of the 17thC, and was common practice from the 18thC onward. The quality of the veneer has a great bearing on the price.

Many early 18thC pieces have quarter-veneered tops – that is, tops laid in four sections of matching veneers. This not only produced a decorative effect but was also practical: until the mid-18thC walnut could not be cut into sufficiently large pieces.

Decorative veneers, or banding, are common on 18thC furniture, usually around the edges of drawer fronts, panels and on table tops, to complement the principal veneer. There are three main types.

1. Cross banding

This is laid in short sections at right angles to the veneered surface, and is usually associated wtih high-quality pieces. It is often used in conjunction with line inlay. Being applied to the edges of pieces, it is prone to lifting and coming away and it is quite common to find areas that have been restored.

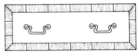

2. Straight banding

This is applied in one long strip, often along a drawer front, and is simpler to apply than cross banding and less prone to lifting or coming away.

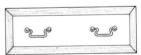

3. Feather or herringbone banding

This type of decoration is associated with the early 18thC and consists of two narrow strips of diagonally banded veneers placed together to give a feather-like appearance. It was particularly popular on early 18thC bureaux and other case furniture.

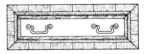

INLAYS

Inlaying involves letting into the surface of a piece of veneered furniture other woods, usually of contrasting colours. (Some early

14

pieces in the solid are occasionally inlaid.) Inlaying was popular on English and Continental furniture of the 17th, 18th and 19thC, and in the United States from the 19thC. The main types are line inlay, marquetry and parquetry.

Line inlay
Also known as stringing, this involves the letting into the surface of narrow lines of one or more woods, usually at the edge or slightly inset. It was especially popular from the end of the Chippendale period.

Marquetry
This is a more elaborate form of line inlay, popular on the Continent of Europe, especially during the 17th and 18thC. It usually includes floral patterns and a wide range of other motifs, such as birds, urns, shells and scrollwork. The condition of any marquetry decoration has a significant bearing on value (see p. 23).

Parquetry
Parquetry involves making a design, often geometric, from small pieces of contrasting veneers. In England it was popular during the second half of the 17thC and again on small early 19thC pieces. Parquetry enjoyed a longer period of popularity in Continental Europe.

Oyster-veneering
A form of parquetry decoration, popular in England and associated with the last quarter of the 17thC, was oyster-veneering – a process of building up a series of small veneers, such as laburnum or cherry, cut from the branches of the tree to produce a highly decorative circular effect.

LACQUERING AND JAPANNING
These forms of decoration were popular on the Continent of Europe during the 16th and 17thC – in France, lacquered panels were often imported from the East and inset into furniture. The fashion came to England during the late 17thC.

The process of lacquering involves laying gum from trees onto the surface of the wood and then applying colour. The most common colours are black and scarlet; green and blue are rare and expensive. The surface is further decorated with gilt highlights, which invariably show chinoiserie scenes.

Japanning, the European version of lacquering, involves building up layers of gesso, polish, and other substances, which are then decorated in the same way as lacquer. Japanning was used to a limited extent in the United States.

PAINTING
The practice of painting oak furniture was common in England during medieval times and in the United States in the 16th and 17thC. Painted furniture enjoyed a revival in England during the late 18thC, when satinwood in particular was highlighted with delicate Neo-classical style paintwork. The Edwardians also favoured painted furniture and decorated much previously unpainted 18thC furniture. Some late 18thC and Regency pieces, especially chairs, are completely decorated.

GILDING
This involves covering or partially gilding (parcel-gilding) a piece with gold leaf. The surface is first prepared with a plaster-like substance known as gesso, and then dampened with water or oil. The gold leaf is applied while the gesso is still sticky. The highlights are sometimes burnished to create a contrasting effect.

In England gilding was first found only on the finest pieces of the 17thC. It was used more extensively during the 18thC, particularly on carved console tables and mirrors and chairs in the French taste. Gilding was also popular throughout Europe, especially in France. In the United States it was not much seen until the 19thC, when it continued to be used extensively throughout Europe.

METAL MOUNTS
Many sophisticated pieces of Continental furniture (and a few English ones) are embellished with applied mounts. On finest items the mounts are ormolu: cast in bronze and then gilded. On poor quality 19thC pieces the mounts are cast in spelter (a base metal). Metal mounts were not used in the United States until the early 19thC, when styles reflected those of the French Empire period.

BASICS (3)

MARRIAGES, IMPROVEMENTS AND FAKES

Marriages

This term is used to describe two- or three-part furniture that has been "made-up" from separate items: large furniture – for example, bureau bookcases, highboys and so on – was often made in two or three pieces, which have subsequently become separated and used individually. The "married" parts may be of the same period, or one part may be later, even relatively modern, and coloured and polished to resemble the older part. The style and proportions, the type of decoration, and the general construction, including the drawers, should all be examined in the way described on pp. 32-3 in order to determine that the components belong together.

Improvements

This is the term given to changes made to a piece of furniture at a later date, either simply to make it more attractive, or to increase its value or saleability by giving it the features of a more desirable item. There are three main types.
1. Alterations to the style or profile of legs to suggest a different, usually earlier period. These can be detected by a difference in the timber used and signs of reworking, and by parts that display fewer signs of age.
2. On tables, reworked tops – for example, "dishing" a tripod table (see p. 97).
3. Later decoration. Cross-bandings and decorative inlays were often added during the Edwardian period to furniture that would never have had such decoration when made.

Alterations in size

Some furniture has been altered in size. Again, this can either be for practical reasons or to increase the value: small furniture is generally more sought-after than large furniture. Such alterations are impossible to disguise completely.
1. Reductions in depth. This practice is most common on bookcases, sideboards and serving tables, and can often be detected by the presence of freshly cut surfaces and by re-made and re-jointed drawers.
2. Reductions in width. This will

involve the repositioning of the handles of any drawers. Plugged holes may be apparent near the edge of the now narrower drawer. Similarly, any locks will have had to be recentred and their original siting patched. The drawers will have had to be re-constructed.
3. Reductions in height, most common on bookcases. This will involve re-constructing the doors and adjusting the glazing bars (see p. 161).

Conversions

Some types of furniture are prone to being converted, their function changed altogether. For example, many highly decorative polescreens have been converted into occasional tables by adding a stem. Some trays have been converted into occasional tables (see p. 179). Another common type of alteration involves removing the commode or pot-cupboard element of commode furniture (see p. 67).

Fakes

This category includes furniture made to deceive. Those fakes made using new timber are relatively easy to detect, but a piece made up using old materials (perhaps from a damaged item), can be very difficult to detect, even for experts. However, fakers usually slip up somewhere and a methodical inspection should reveal an element that is not "right". Specific types of fakes are dealt with throughout the book, but there are a few telltale signs common to many fakes especially where the carcass has been veneered or reveneered.
1. If an old oak piece has been veneered up with walnut the old oak mouldings will have had to be replaced with newly made and distressed walnut mouldings.
2. Decorative details, such as stringing and other inlays, which have been added to an old carcass may not show the usual signs of age – for example, on genuine early walnut there is usually a fine dark seam around the stringing and at the joints of veneer where the sap has seeped out of the wood from seams and attracted dirt over the years.
3. The veneer may show signs of old handles or escutcheons in positions that do not correspond with any new fixtures.
4. There may be signs of damage

that has been repaired. For example, there should be visible evidence on both the inside and outside of any breaks or splits. If a split is visible only on the inside and the outer veneered (or lacquered) surface is unblemished, the veneer or lacquer has almost certainly been applied at a later date.
5. There may be evidence inside the drawers of plugged or unplugged handle holes, but not outside – again, a sign of later veneering.

CONDITION

Antique furniture in pristine condition is increasingly hard to come by and commands the highest prices. However, a category of furniture often overlooked includes genuine, attractive pieces which, though not in perfect condition, could be fully restored by a professional polisher or restorer. Fine-quality furniture has generally survived better than that of poorer quality and can usually be more satisfactorily restored. With experience, the collector will learn to distinguish between the various types of minor restoration and more complex or specialist work, which can be very expensive.

Polished surfaces
Uneven fading and worn polish are common problems and if serious can cause a piece to look beyond redemption. Fading usually occurs as a result of furniture standing in the same, possibly sunny spot for a number of years. A piece may also fade unevenly, perhaps because something solid has stood on it for a long period, preventing light from reaching the covered area. Polished surfaces can also be spoiled by watermarks and other stains that result from natural wear and tear. Direct sunlight over a period of time causes polish to chip away and perish. However, as long as the wood itself is in good condition and free of gouges and splits, stripping and repolishing can restore any piece to its original condition.

Restoration
Restoration is a factor which will have a bearing on the price, so it is important to establish the degree (if any) of restoration that

a piece has undergone – this will involve careful observation. Acceptable restoration includes:
* minor repairs to bandings and mouldings
* reupholstery or replacement of silk panels, and re-leathering
* repolishing
* replacement of incorrect handles with ones that are stylistically correct
* tightening of joints, drawer linings, backs and so on
* re-bushed casters.

There may also be areas where a substantial degree of restoration has been carried out or is necessary. However, this should be reflected in the price. The main types include:
* bad warping of table tops, panels, and so on
* replaced legs or tops
* replaced drawers or panels
* whole sections that have been re-veneered
* refashioned glazing bars
* total redecoration of painted furniture.

Care
To maintain its condition – and its value – antique furniture should be properly cared for.
* Think about the temperature and the humidity of the room the furniture is to stand in – for example, close contact with radiators is best avoided, especially if the piece has brass inlay, as this can pop out. Very dry and very damp conditions may also have adverse effects, causing furniture to warp or split.
* Avoid silicone polishes as these are generally harmful to antique furniture. Use a wax polish and a soft dry cloth.
* Treat pieces with respect: pick them up rather than drag them and avoid subjecting them to unneccessary strain. Avoid using carrying handles, as these are sometimes more decorative than functional.

Woodworm
Signs of old woodworm infestation need not deter the prospective purchaser provided that it is inactive and that the degree of infestation has not structurally weakened the piece. Periodic checks should be made. Active woodworm can be detected by pale white powder in the worm holes or on the floor nearby.

CHESTS AND CUPBOARDS

The coffer, basically an oak box raised up on stiles, with a hinged lid, was the earliest form of furniture. From it evolved more sophisticated forms of chest, and settles, from which chairs derive.

A few 13thC coffers have survived, although these are mostly museum or church pieces. They are of very basic construction and consist of nailed planks sometimes reinforced with iron bandings. By the 17thC coffers were made in large numbers and were of joined and panelled construction, usually with some carved decoration. The degree and quality of carving have a significant bearing on the price. Coffers are still in plentiful supply today and good examples can be purchased for modest sums. Coffers and press cupboards were also made in the United States. The Jacobean style is seen throughout the 17thC, and new forms began to appear alongside it from c.1675.

The court cupboard or buffet was popular during the 17thC in both open and enclosed form. The open type was used as a cupboard and also as a means of displaying valuable possessions, such as pewter vessels and Oriental china. Victorian imitations tend to be stained very dark, and lack the glowing patina of the originals.

In the mid-17thC the coffer evolved into the mule chest, which had a drawer at the base to make it easier to gain access to items stored at the bottom. By the end of the 17thC the mule chest had in turn evolved into the chest of drawers with a fixed top, now made by a cabinet-maker rather than a joiner. At this period chests were made principally in oak or walnut and raised on bun feet. Increasingly toward the end of the 17thC they were either wholly veneered in walnut or oyster-veneered in laburnum or cherry.

The 18thC English chest is generally plainer than that of the 17thC. The best examples are in burr walnut, and may have a brushing slide. From c.1700 most are on bracket feet. Many are cross- or feather-banded. Good small examples from this period, with an old surface, are becoming very rare and command extraordinarily high prices.

Chests-on-stands and chests-on-chests (known in the United States as highboys and tallboys respectively) were introduced in the William and Mary and Queen Anne periods and in the United States some twenty years later. The highboy was one of the most important pieces of American furniture, and remained popular throughout the American Chippendale period. The simplest type consists basically of one square chest placed on top of another, which gives a somewhat box-like effect. Better examples will have canted sides to the upper section (and sometimes to the lower section as well).

The Queen Anne period also saw the introduction of the "bachelor" chest – a small shallow walnut chest with a folding top supported by pull-out lopers. These are highly priced today but beware – a high percentage of those on the market are fakes.

By the mid-18thC most chests are in mahogany, either veneered or solid, and stand on bracket or ogee bracket feet. Drawer edges are cock-beaded (see p. 13).

Later in the 18thC greater emphasis was placed on lighter designs, heavily influenced by elegant French forms, such as the serpentine commode raised on slender cabriole legs. Crossbanding and marquetry inlay of Neo-classical design, including swags, rams' heads, festoons and so on, were popular. Mahogany continued to be used, but more in figured or veneered form than previously. Exotic woods, such as satinwood and kingwood, were commonly used. Some high-fashion examples have applied ormolu mounts.

The bow-fronted shape became popular in the late 18thC and was the main Regency form, especially in the United States, where it was particularly ornate. In England the bow-fronted chest is associated with the splayed French-style foot. American examples are often raised on turned supports.

Although the chest-on-chest had declined in popularity by the end of the 18thC, the linen press (see pp. 38-9) continued to be popular well into the 19thC, before being superseded by the full-length wardrobe.

During the Victorian period walnut veneer replaced mahogany as the main wood for fashionable pieces. Robust wardrobes were made in a variety of styles, some with mirrored doors. As well as essentially Victorian forms of chest there were also many revivals, of which Chippendale-period commodes were perhaps the most popular. The Edwardian period saw a return to lighter styles, although large wardrobes continued to be in demand.

Unlike some other categories of furniture, such as circular dining tables, the smaller the chest is, the more desirable it is likely to be – provided of course, that it is of high quality. Decorative details, such as canted corners and architectural pediments, will boost the price considerably.

Examining a chest of drawers is a useful way to start learning how to assess antique furniture, as the basic procedure is relevant to many pieces. First, assess the type and quality of the timber, the overall proportions and method of construction – if it is joined (see p. 12) then it is probably earlier than 1700 – if not, probably later. Then remove the drawers and see how they are constructed and finished (see p. 13), and examine the style of feet and handles to establish whether they are original or later replacements (see pp. 26-7 and 110-13). While the drawers are out look inside the carcass to ascertain that there are no signs of disturbance or inexplicable marks. Similarly, examine the back and underside. This methodical examination, which can be applied to most drawered pieces, should help you feel confident that you have not overlooked any major flaws.

COFFERS

A late 17thC English oak coffer
c.1680; ht 27in/68.5cm, wdth 54in/138.5cm; value range E-F

Identification checklist for 17thC coffers
1. Is the coffer oak?
2. Is it of joined, panel and frame construction? (See p. 12 and Variations, *below.*)
3. Is it carved?
4. Is the carving contemporary with the coffer, that is, in a bold free style, with a build-up of dirt and wax in the crevices?
5. Are the pegs hand-made, that is, irregularly shaped and standing slightly proud of the surface?
6. Are the panels and stiles original (see Condition)?
7. Does the coffer retain its original hinges and lock?

Signs of quality
This coffer has several good features:
* panelling to the top as well as to the sides
* moulded rather than plain stiles
* attractively carved original frieze, and side carving.

Coffers
Coffers were made over a long period, with many local variations. In the 15th and 16thC they were made for churches and cathedrals, and were massive. Many were of boarded construction, and iron-bound. These are now very scarce. The example shown *above* is typical of later coffers, made in quantity from the 17thC, and is of the type usually found today.
20

.Variations
* Simpler versions have a joined or nailed plank top and sides and a boarded back.
* Sizes vary, but this is not usually a factor in the price.
* American coffers are often found in cherry.

Carving
The carving, which consists of lozenges, rosettes and foliate motifs, is original to the piece. The Victorians often added carving to plain early oak furniture, and also reproduced earlier styles, complete with carving. However, Victorian carving is laboured and machine-like and lacks the patination and highlights of original old carving.

Colour

The coffer (*left*) is a rich colour, and has developed a fine patina. The top is darker around the edges where it has overhung the base (particularly at the sides, where the overhang is greater).
* The inside of the coffer should be even in colour, and have a dry undisturbed look.
* The top panels of coffers are prone to splitting. Unless the split is beyond repair, or a panel has been replaced, the value will not be seriously reduced.

Condition

The panelled oak coffer *above*, c.1670-85, with original carving, makes an instructive comparison with that shown opposite. Though similar in style and date, it has several replacement parts, which seriously reduce its value. The top has replaced panels inside the lid (see *right*): these can be detected by the presence of fresh glue and more importantly, by the generally new appearance of the wood – this does not match the rest of the piece, and has some unaccountable marks, suggesting that it was taken from another, perhaps badly damaged, piece of furniture. The replaced hinges are less detrimental to value, although it would be

preferable to have the original ring ones. The stile feet are in relatively good condition for their age. It is not uncommon for such feet to be repaired or cut down to even them up if they are badly worn. Replacement stiles, which are more detrimental to value than repaired originals, will be in a different wood and may have a generally newer appearance than the rest of the coffer.

COURT CUPBOARDS

A late 17thC English oak court cupboard
c.1680; ht 4ft 7in/140cm; wdth 4ft 6in/137cm; value range C–E.

Identification checklist for 17thC court cupboards
1. Is the piece oak?
2. Is it of joined construction, and the back secured with hand-made nails (see p. 12)?
3. Are the pegs hand-made (irregular and standing proud of the surface)?
4. Are the dovetails of the drawers fairly crude and the drawer linings thick – approx. $5/8$in/1.5cm?
5. Is the carving contemporary – of a free style with a build-up of dirt and wax in the crevices?
6. Do the doors open on pin hinges?
7. Do the timber and any mouldings or decorative features match on both halves?

Court cupboards

This type of furniture was first seen in England c.1550 and continued to be made during the 18thC, especially in Wales. Most court cupboards available today date from the 17thC, in particular from the latter part. They vary in size. The example shown here is very small, and thus very desirable. Those from the north of England can be as wide as 8ft (24m). They are not prone to being married or faked. Prices have recently begun to rise.

Signs of quality

The court cupboard *above* has a number of features that enhance its desirability:
* inlaid panels on the upper section
* well-carved friezes to top and bottom sections
* punch-carved stiles, doors and side panels
* excellent patination and fine colour
* original candle shelf – on court cupboards these are often replaced.

Marquetry

Some of the marquetry flowers have been restored. This is to be expected from a piece of this age, and therefore will not seriously affect the value. Although some areas have been completely replaced, a significant amount of the original work remains.

* It is possible to assess the age of marquetry decoration relative to the age of the piece by running your fingers along its surface: if it is totally flat, it is probably a recent replacement. Old marquetry decoration has a softly undulating surface caused by the shrinkage of the boards beneath it.

* A plugged hole is visible to the side of the handle where the original turned knobs were situated.

* Some marquetry decoration, especially from the 19thC, is of somewhat indifferent quality: leaves and other motifs should be well-drawn with fine detail (see pp. 34-5.)

Doors

Over the years the doors have dropped slightly on their pin hinges, leaving a gap when the door is closed between the top of the door and the frame. This detail from one of the lower doors of the court cupboard shows how the gap has been built up using graduated slivers of wood. This is a necessary and therefore acceptable repair.

* Dropped doors, whether built up or not, do at least indicate that they are likely to be original to the piece.

Construction and condition

Court cupboards are always made in two aligned sections. Check that the mouldings follow through from the top to the bottom, as they do on this piece. Small quantities of replaced moulding are acceptable. The timber and any carving should match on both sections.

* Early court cupboards had balusters going all the way through. Drop finials are a later feature, introduced around the middle of the 17thC. They vary in shape from region to region. Very late pendants have an almost emaciated look.

* Ideally, the panels should all be original. A replaced side panel does not devalue the piece nearly as much as replaced carved or inlaid front panels, even if the replacements are stylistically faithful to the originals. A replaced panel should be apparent on close inspection: the grain and patination of the original timber would be impossible to match exactly. Some of the panels on this piece have been somewhat overcleaned and have lost their patination as a result. The split in the panel of this piece, though visible (see detail *above*), at least is on the side rather than the front.

* There is likely to be some splitting of the base boards, and some repaired or even replaced back boards (which will not match the others in type of wood and colour). This is of minor concern to a potential buyer.

* Stiles are often built up. This is perfectly acceptable in furniture of this age which will have stood on damp floors for long periods.

An English walnut chest on bun feet
late 17thC; 37in/94cm, wdth 42in/106.5cm; value range D-F

Identification checklist for late 17thC chests
1. Is the chest oak or walnut?
2. Is it solid (as opposed to veneered)?
3. Has it been made using the joined style of construction?
4. Has it moulded drawer fronts?
5. Do the drawers have chunky oak or pine linings and bold, relatively crude dovetailing?
6. Do the drawers have side runners?
7. Does the grain of the drawer bottoms run from front to back?
8. Does the chest have its original bun feet?

17thC chests
Drawered chests evolved in the 17thC from panelled coffers (see pp. 20-21). Until the late 17thC they were made in the solid, usually in oak or walnut, by the joined method of construction, using mortice and tenon joints, and held by pegs or dowels.

Colour
Some variation in tone is to be expected: wood fades when exposed to light over a long period. A side is likely to be less faded than a top, which will have received more light. Individual surfaces may also be uneven in colour where dirt has built up on the mouldings.

Tops
Tops of early pieces are made with two or more planks of wood. These often show gaps caused by shrinkage. Large gaps or splits are sometimes infilled.

Feet
Bun feet, like those of the chest shown here, were popular in the late 17thC. As many as 95% of those found today are replacements – walnut is a soft wood, susceptible to woodworm and rot. Replacements do not greatly reduce value provided that they have been well-turned in walnut, correctly proportioned, and coloured and polished to match the rest of the piece.

Drawers
The drawer fronts of 17thC chests
usually have applied decorative
mouldings (as opposed to 18thC
chests, which tend to be plain
with simple moulding or beading
around the edges). In the 17thC
the boards are laid so that the
grain of the drawer bottoms runs
from front to back.

Channels
The sides of the drawers are
typically thick. This is because
the drawers of 17thC chests
commonly move backwards and
forwards on side runners. These
are fitted within the carcass of the
chest and slot into the channels
cut into the sides of the drawers.
(For comparison see 18thC chests,
pp. 28-9.)
* The pegs are hand-made.
Chests of this age sometimes have
a few replacement pegs which
will be machine-made, but be
suspicious if all the pegs are
modern (see p. 12).

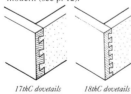

17thC dovetails   *18thC dovetails*

Dovetails
The drawers of 17thC chests
usually have three fairly coarse
dovetails (the joints at the corners
where the pieces have been
slotted together, see p. 12). A later
piece may have five or six finer
ones. Check that the dovetailing
of each drawer corresponds with
the rest.

Value points
* Small chests are worth more
than large ones of similar quality.
* Provided it is of good colour, a
walnut chest is considered more
desirable than an oak one.

Handles
The handle of the chest shown
here is, typically, held in place
with the split pin method: the
pommel is pushed through the
drawer, then split open to secure
the handle (*above, top*). These
handles are clearly the originals:
there are no marks on the back or
front of the drawer to suggest that
other handles have been fixed
there. Confirmation of their
authenticity is provided by the
indentation on the wood caused
by the handle swinging against it
over the years (*above, bottom*).
There is also a natural build-up of
dirt and wax in the crevices,
indicative of age.

The carcass
Backs are not polished or finely
finished. They usually have three
or four backboards, sometimes
chamfered off around the edges,
and roughly nailed onto the
carcass.
* The underside will be dry,
roughly hewn and unfinished and,
like the top, may well have splits,
caused by shrinkage and natural
defects in the wood, a process
hastened by central heating.
Splits inside the carcass are not a
problem unless they are very
deep.

25

HANDLES AND ESCUTCHEONS

Late 17th/early 18thC

Early 18thC

2nd quarter 18thC

3rd quarter 18thC

Late 18th/early 19thC

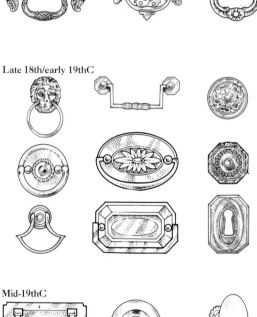

Mid-19thC

Late 19thC

18THC CHESTS

An English George III mahogany chest of drawers
c.1760; ht 35in/89cm, wdth 37in/94cm; value range D-F

Identification checklist for 18thC chests of drawers
1. Is the chest mahogany?
2. Does it have bracket (or ogee bracket) feet?
3. Do the drawers have five or six fine dovetails (the joints at the corners where the pieces have been slotted together)?
4. Are the drawers lined in oak or pine?
5. Are the drawer linings relatively fine, approx. ¹/₄in (0.5cm)?
6. Are the drawer fronts either overlapping or cock-beaded (see p. 13)?
7. Does the piece retain its original swan-neck handles, secured with circular nuts?

18thC chests
From c.1740 chests are usually mahogany and were either made in the solid or are veneered, as this one is. The top is usually veneered in one piece (rather than quartered – see p. 14). Until the mid-18thC, backs were still roughly finished and unpolished. From the second half of the century more attention was paid to finishing the back, often using a panelled form of construction. However, it was still left unpolished. The backs of high-quality pieces are generally held in place with countersunk screws.

The example *above* has the standard 18thC form, but is particularly fine, with several additional and desirable features not found on more basic or provincially made chests of the period:
* brushing slide (the pull-out slide above the drawers)
* ogee bracket feet (rather than the more typical bracket foot shown on the opposite page)
* canted (angled) corners to the top and sides of the chest.

Drawers

Drawer fronts are better finished than in the 17thC and are either neatly finished off with overlapping ovolo (quarter-round) moulding, or, usually from c.1725, with a beaded moulding known as cockbeading, as in the example here. Drawer dividers are now plain. Drawer linings, which are either oak or mahogany, or occasionally, pine, became progressively finer during the 18thC: the standard width is approx 1/4in (0.5cm). From the early 18thC the runners were placed underneath the drawer, at the sides, and ran on bearers placed along the inside of the carcass.

Handles

The handles are stylistically correct for the period and close inspection confirms that they are original to the piece: there are no suspicious marks on the drawer fronts to indicate that other handles have been there. This can be confirmed by examining the back of the drawer, which should look undisturbed (see *below*).

Locks

The back of the drawer front looks as it should – it is unpolished and undisturbed, apart from a few knocks and scuffs. The lock is original – it is a snug fit and is fixed with old steel screws.
* The channels on either side of the lock indicate that the drawer was originally sectioned: top drawers were often divided into compartments for make-up and so on, and sometimes contained a mirror which pulled out on a ratchet device. In theory, chests that retain these features command a premium, but many people find those without more convenient.

Dating point

Grain running from side to side in the drawer bottoms (rather than from front to back) indicates a date of c.1780 or later.

Value points

* The walnut chests made in the early 18thC are generally more expensive than 18thC mahogany chests, which were made in far greater numbers.
* Smaller chests are generally more desirable than larger ones.

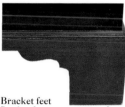

Bracket feet

Bracket feet were common from the beginning of the 18thC and were used until the early 19thC. Approximately 50 percent of those found today are replacements. The bracket foot *above* (from another 18thC chest) is stylistically correct for the period, and on first inspection appears to be original to the piece: the colour match is good and there are no obvious signs of disturbance.

On closer inspection from the underside it becomes apparent that the foot shown *above* is a replacement, although sensitively fitted: the timber is relatively new and although stained to look old, nevertheless lacks the signs of ageing apparent elsewhere on the underside.
* All the blocks on which the feet are mounted should be similar in appearance.

CHESTS-ON-CHESTS

An English mahogany chest-on-chest
c.1750; ht 74in/188cm, wdth 41in/104cm; value range C-F

Identification checklist for mid-18thC chests-on-chests
(tallboys)
1. Is the piece mahogany?
2. Is it partly veneered and partly in the solid?
3. Does it have bracket feet?
4. Are the drawers cock-beaded?
5. Does the piece have carved decoration?
6. Does it have a brushing slide?
7. Do both sections retain their original, matching swan-neck handles?
8. Is the style of construction the same for all the drawers in both parts?
9. Do any decorative details match on both parts?

Dating points
Several features identify the chest-on-chest *above* as mid-18thC:
* bold bracket feet below the base moulding. Later examples may have splayed bracket feet
* blind fretwork carving to the canted corners (fluting was a popular alternative). On earlier pieces canted corners would have carved rather than inlaid decoration
* the style of the swan-neck handles. Swan-necks were popular all through the second half of the 18thC.

Chests-on-chests

Chests-on-chests, or tallboys, were first made in the late 17th/early 18thC, when they were usually in walnut with feather banding, overlapping drawer mouldings and bun or bracket feet. They were invariably in two sections with a cornice. A few had a concave inlaid sunburst set into the bottom drawer and these are particularly sought-after today. From the mid-1730s they were more usually in mahogany, either in the solid, or veneered, as this one is, giving a more highly figured appearance. Chippendale-period mahogany examples often have an architectural pediment. Country versions were made in oak throughout the period of production. A few tallboys exist in other timbers, such as yew. The best and most desirable tallboys belong to the early 18thC and the Chippendale period. They were far less common after c.1780, and had virtually ceased to be made after the first quarter of the 19thC.

Quality features

The value of this example is enhanced by its:
* brushing slide
* pierced decoration on the feet
* blind fretwork carving.

Married chests-on-chests

Chests-on-chests, along with other two- (and three-) part pieces of furniture, are prone to being married, that is, made up from different pieces of furniture which may not even be of the same period as each other. Certain checks can be made to establish that the components of a piece belong together. Stand back and look at the overall style and proportions. It is generally possible to tell – for example, where a top looks too heavy for its base: a top should be slightly narrower than the base it sits on. If the parts are of exactly the same width, or if the width difference is very marked, the piece may well look clumsy or awkward. Next, compare the two halves from the front: the colour of the timber and the veneers should match on both parts, as they do on this piece. Then, compare the colour of the sides and the construction of the .drawers on both parts (see *right*).'

Drawers

The drawers on both parts should match each other in terms of style and construction. These drawers correspond in every respect: they have the same oak base and linings, and the dovetails are of the same thickness. Small slivers of wood have been added to counteract a degree of shrinkage in the boards inevitable on furniture of this age.

Sides

Discrepancies in colour or style are sometimes easier to detect from the side of the piece rather than from the front. However, you should expect some difference in colour, as the top half is likely to have received more light than the lower half and may therefore be paler, as has happened with this tallboy. This top sits on the base within an applied moulding. Separate the parts and check that the top of the base reveals the marks made by any bearers on the underside of the top section, and that any other marks correspond with each other.
* The backboards are of matching wood. A strip of hessian on tape soaked in glue has been applied to correct bowing or shrinkage; this is an accepted method of repair.

31

CABINETS-ON-CHESTS

An early 18thC English walnut cabinet-on-chest
c.1720; ht 71in/185cm; wdth 60in/152cm; value range C-E.

Identification checklist for early 18thC cabinets-on-chests
1. Is the piece walnut?
2. Is it veneered?
3. Does it have characteristic half-round mouldings?
4. Does it have carrying handles?
5. Are the drawers feather-banded?
6. Do the sides have inlaid decorative details?
7. Does the piece have bracket feet of simple profile?
8. Do the drawers have oak or pine linings?
9. Do the top and bottom belong together (see Marriages)?

Cabinets-on-chests
The cabinet-on-chest evolved during the last years of the 17thC and was popular throughout the walnut period. It was the forerunner of the linen press (see pp. 38-9). The typical example *above*, has faded to a particularly charming pale colour.

Authenticity
As with chests-on-chests and

highboys, cabinets-on-chests are prone to being married, that is, made up of two separate pieces of furniture not intended to be together, and not even necessarily of the same period, and they should be examined for signs of authenticity in the same way (see pp. 30-31). Compare the "right" piece above with the "wrong" or "married" piece on the facing page.

Feather banding
A comparison of the feather banding (see p. 14) on the two parts reveals a subtle difference: on the top part of the married cabinet-on-chest the feathering on the left-hand door points to the left, while that on the right-hand door points to the right. This is not reflected in the bottom section, as it would have been had the two pieces been made at the same time.

Married cabinets-on-chests
The late 17thC walnut veneered cabinet-on-chest *above*, makes an instructive comparison with that shown on the previous page, as it is a marriage between two pieces not originally intended to go together. There are a number of unmistakeable clues:
* The cabinet is a little heavy in appearance for the chest base. The genuine piece on the previous page is perfectly proportioned.
* The veneers have clearly not been cut from the same piece of timber, as they would have been on pieces that belong with each other. The quality of veneer on the cabinet, with its figuring and swirls, is clearly superior to the veneers of the chest base. Also, the chest lacks the patination and warm glow of the cabinet, although the pieces are reasonably well-matched in terms of colour.
* The waist moulding between the cabinet and chest is flush with the base on the front but overhangs on the side. If the pieces had been designed to go together the overhang would be the same at the sides as at the front.
* Although it is perfectly acceptable for the upper section of a two-part piece to be a cabinet while the lower section is a chest, there should not be differences in any decorative detailing, although there are here, see right. Any internal drawers in the cabinet should match those of the chest in style of construction and decoration.

Detecting later inlay
When pieces are married it is sometimes necessary to add decorative details to one of the parts: if this has happened it will be possible to detect areas where the knife has cut into the veneer and torn the edges: it is difficult when inlaying a piece at a later date to cut into veneer that has already been glued down onto the ground wood.

Assembly
The way in which the cabinet sits on the chest is also indicative of a marriage. Had the parts been designed together, the cabinet would have sat on bearers running along the side and front edges of the chest, resulting in lighter patches where the air would not have reached the carcass. However, this piece shows no indication of having had bearers. The detail *above* shows marks on the top of the lower section where another piece has sat on it: these marks do not correspond with any that could have been made by the top section.
* The backboards of both sections should be of the same wood, and similarly constructed and fitted – for example, backboards are sometimes recessed.

MARQUETRY CABINETS

An 18thC Dutch walnut marquetry cabinet
3rd quarter of the 18thC; ht 90^{1}/$_{2}$in/230cm, wdth 68in/173cm; value range B-C

Identification checklist for 18thC Dutch marquetry cabinets

1. Is the piece walnut?
2. Does it have all-over marquetry decoration?
3. Does it have applied carved decoration?
4. Does it have cast handles with matching escutcheons?
5. Is the base of bombé shape?
6. Does the piece have massively carved ebonized feet?
7. Is the top section held together with internal pegs (see facing page)?
8. Is the top of panelled construction?
9. Does the piece have plateaux on the cornice for ornaments?

Dutch marquetry chests and cabinets

The cabinet was an important piece of Dutch furniture, betokening status – the larger and more impressive the cabinet, the wealthier and more important its owner was deemed to be. The example *above* is particularly fine, exhibiting workmanship of the highest quality, and will command a premium.

Marquetry decoration

Marquetry decoration was popular with Dutch cabinet-makers from the early 17thC and throughout the 18th and 19thC. In England marquetry was employed to its greatest extent during the second half of the 17thC. In the 17th and 18thC the quality of marquetry was high, but had declined markedly by the 19thC (see *opposite page*).

Typical features

The cabinet in the main picture exhibits a number of features typical of Dutch furniture of the period:
* the bombé base (rarely found on English furniture)
* the cast handles
* the applied carved details, which here include urns
* the shaped apron (usually on quality pieces).
This type of cabinet is also found simply veneered in walnut (see *below right*).

Construction

Being of unusually large proportions, these cabinets are constructed using tenons and pegs and are made in several sections. The pegs are simply knocked in rather than glued in the usual manner of the period. Thus they can be removed to enable the whole of the upper part, including the sides, doors, cornice and panel back, to be dismantled. The back, which is left unpolished, occasionally divides into two sections.

Quality of marquetry

When a section of the marquetry work from the cabinet (*above left*) is compared with a section from the chest (*above right*), the difference in quality is readily apparent: the marquetry work of the cabinet, which incorporates Classical urns, floral displays, songbirds and butterflies, is lively and finely detailed, whereas that of the chest lacks a sense of movement and is stiff and rather crudely drawn.
* The highly-figured veneers employed on the cabinet complement the marquetrywork, especially on the doors.

Later Continental cabinets

The bombé style of chest with marquetry decoration was reproduced in Holland during the 19thC with the basic design and feet being identical to that of 18thC pieces. However, the example illustrated *above* aptly shows the difference in the quality and effect of the decoration when compared with the cabinet shown on the previous page. The veneers employed here are of indifferent quality. The handles are poorly cast and from the way they have worn it is evident that they have been cheaply gilded. However, the most striking difference between the pieces is in the quality of the marquetry work, see *above right*.

Plainer Dutch cabinets

Mid-18thC Dutch cabinets-on-chests are also found plainly veneered, as this one is. It lacks the heavily carved detailing of the grander marquetry-decorated cabinets, and although well-made, will be worth approximately half the value of its more elaborate counterpart.
* Walnut was still employed extensively in Holland during the mid-18thC although it had ceased to be used much in England at this period.

A small 18thC English mahogany standing corner cupboard of bow-fronted design c.1785; ht 70in/178cm; value range D-F

Identification checklist for 18thC standing corner cupboards
1. Is the cupboard mahogany?
2. Is it constructed in two sections?
3. Do the sections match each other in terms of decorative details, method of construction, and so on?
4. Does the cupboard have its original bracket feet?
5. Does it have reeded decoration down the sides?
6. If glazed, are the glazing bars stylistically correct for the period (see p. 161)?

Corner cupboards

Corner cupboards were very popular during the 18thC. They were made in two basic forms, either hanging or standing; the standing variety was usually made in two sections, one simply sitting on the other, and held together with screws. Blind doors (solid rather than glazed) were used until the mid-18thC; both blind and glazed doors were used after that date. Corner cupboards were made in a variety of timbers, which were either polished or lacquered: walnut from the early 18thC, mahogany from the 1730s; oak and fruitwoods were used in provincial examples throughout the period of production. During the second half of the 18thC the bow-fronted type became very popular, especially in hanging form, usually with two doors. Most standing corner cupboards are straight-fronted. They vary in size from the sort of dimensions of that shown *opposite*, up to very large architectural types with applied pilasters, broken pediments and so on.

Authenticity

Marriages are uncommon, but it is worth checking that the sections belong with one another, as those of the cupboard in the main picture clearly do: both have matching mouldings and decoration. Matching hinges will have been used for both parts.

Glazing

Some cupboards have had their blind doors replaced by glazed ones: the glazing bars, or astragals, should look old and undisturbed. Some replacement glass is to be expected (see p. 161).

Construction

From the inside of the top section the fixing screws used to hold the two parts together are clearly visible. There should only be corresponding holes in the base section – others (not corresponding with the top) may indicate that the piece is "married" (see p. 16-17).

Lacquered corner cupboards

Bow-fronted corner cupboards with lacquer, like the hanging example, *above*, from c.1770, usually have chinoiserie decoration. This one is in remarkably good condition: lacquer is easily chipped, and usually shows signs of having suffered from changes in temperature.
* Green is an unusual colour for a lacquer ground: black is far more common.

Condition

The secondary wood of the lacquered corner cupboard is pine, which has been painted. The backboards, *above*, have split and opened up, and being softwood, have shrunk. Tape soaked in glue and applied to the back is a standard method of stabilizing such boards.
* The backboards of hanging cupboards are often peppered with holes where they have been screwed into the wall.

LINEN PRESSES

A late 18thC English mahogany linen press
c.1785-90; ht 78in/198cm, wdth 50in/127cm; value range D-F

Identification checklist for late 18thC linen presses
1. Is the linen press in veneered mahogany?
2. Is it constructed in two sections with a detachable cornice?
3. Does it stand on its original bracket feet? (A number at this date have splayed bracket feet.)
4. Do the doors have applied moulding?
5. Does the bottom section have either two or three rows of drawers?
6. Are the drawer fronts cock-beaded?
7. Is the cornice either flat or of architectural form?
8. Do the veneers on the sides of the top and bottom sections correspond (see p. 31)?
Note
The handles are likely to be original rather than later replacements (and therefore a good aid to dating), perhaps because linen presses were not high-fashion items in need of "updating".

Decoration

Dramatic use has been made of flamed veneers, now faded to a pleasant pale colour. The corners are inlaid with paterae, *above*, in scorched boxwood (sycamore or box stained green) and harewood.
* A less desirable (and less expensive) type of linen press would be plain, without the decorative veneers or mouldings.
* In the early Chippendale period paterae are carved mahogany and applied.

Linen presses

Linen presses were introduced c.1750. Until 1780 many were in mahogany. Some Victorian presses are veneered in satinwood or walnut. Essentially practical bedroom pieces rather than decorative drawing room ones, and made for all types of households, quality varies dramatically: some are highly sophisticated with fine carving or, from the end of the 18thC, inlays; others are simply constructed and unadorned.

Value

For many years linen presses were extremely undervalued, especially during the 1950s and 60s, when fitted wardrobes were favoured. By the mid-70s they were considered good value, and prices have been rising steadily ever since.

Doors

The doors of linen presses are prone to warping and splitting, as they are made of large expanses of relatively thin timber. From the front the door of this press shows signs of splitting in the panels on the right side, which accounts for the presence of newer strengthening bars, *above*, added on the inside to counteract warping and further splitting.

Interiors

The interior of this press, *above*, was originally fitted with sliding trays, which have been removed and replaced by a bar for hanging clothes. To do this, the base has had to be cut away and the linings of the drawers have been removed – significant alterations which will devalue the piece.

39

SIDE CABINETS

*A Regency-period English mahogany side cabinet
c.1810; ht 33in/84cm; value range B-E*

Identification checklist for Regency side cabinets
1. Is the cabinet mahogany?
2. Does it have any applied brass mouldings or brass inlay?
3. Does it have boldly carved lion's-paw feet?
4. Does it have any of the classic Regency motifs – for example, rope twists, or Egyptian masks or motifs?
5. Does it have any decorative inlay or crossbanding?
6. Are the screws hand-made (see p. 12)?

Side cabinets
Side cabinets were first seen in England during the last quarter of the 18thC. They are found in a variety of sophisticated woods such as satinwood, coromandel or kingwood, but are most commonly in mahogany (sometimes combined with satinwood) or rosewood.

Recognition points
The cabinet *above* has a number of typical Regency features:
* Egyptian motifs; sphinx heads were particularly favoured
* rope twist mouldings on the panelled doors
* ivory inlaid escutcheons; oval

and diamond shapes were also popular.

Alterations
From the late 18thC there was a fashion for doors inset with silk-pleated panels with brass grilles in front (see pp. 164-5). Some cabinets have had their panels removed and replaced by silk. As the silk type is generally more popular, and gives a more sophisticated and lighter look, it is unlikely that any silk panels would have been converted to wooden panels. Nevertheless, it is worth checking that the wood of any panels matches the colour and grain of the rest of the piece.

Victorian side cabinets

Feet
As long as they are original, the style of the feet is very useful in helping to determine the age of a piece. The feet of this cabinet are clearly original: the colour matches that of the rest of the piece, the mouldings at the top of the feet are echoed around the edge of the carcass, a mark is visible where the feet have been tenoned into the block, they have attracted dirt over the years and have also suffered from knocks and scrapes – some of the surface has chipped away, revealing the natural colour of the mahogany beneath. Further evidence of age is provided by the curved marks on the moulding below the doors where the feet of the Egyptian motif scrape across the moulding as the door is opened.

In the 1850s and 60s one of the many styles of side cabinet in vogue was the Italianate style, exemplified by this ornate early Victorian ormolu-mounted *pietra dura* side cabinet. This is a fine example, with several typical features, including:
* the use of ebony veneers
* marble top
* applied mouldings.
The base wood is probably pine – which sometimes shows through in worn areas, such as at the base of the feet.
* Cabinets in this basic design were also made with all over Boulle-style inlay (see p. 180).

Condition
Pietra dura furniture is particularly prone to the kinds of damage listed below.
* The applied decoration is often in poor condition – cast mouldings are pinned on and frequently come away.
* Some discoloration may occur, such as is visible in the side panel of this example.
* The marble tops are fragile and are often replaced. Lift the top off and examine the underside: on an original top this will be dirty, and where it overhangs the base, will be considerably darker and dirtier than the area which covers the base. A newly replaced top will have an unblemished surface and will be free of signs of dirt and wear.
* Missing mounts are expensive to replace, as moulds will have to be taken from any remaining mounts.
* Missing pieces in the *pietra dura* panels will also affect the price.

Signs of age
As well as the feet, other parts of the cabinet may yield reassuring signs of age and authenticity. The hinges and screws of this piece are clearly hand-made, indicative of a date prior to c.1830. Any nails visible – for example, those holding the pine back, should also be hand-made. Other places that may show signs of age are the bottom mouldings, which are prone to being chipped and knocked; and the door panels which often suffer from shrinkage, causing splits.

41

BOW-FRONTED CHESTS

*A late 18thC English mahogany bow-fronted chest
c. 1790; ht 35in/89cm, wdth 33in/85cm; value range D-F*

Identification checklist for late 18th/early 19thC bow-fronted chests

1. Is the chest mahogany? (Satinwood and bird's eye maple were also used occasionally.)
2. Is it veneered?
3. Does it have splayed bracket feet?
4. Do the drawer linings have the fine dovetailing typical of the late 18th/early 19thC?
5. Are the drawer linings in oak or mahogany? (Pine is used for lesser examples.)
6. Do the baseboards of the drawers run from the sides into the middle and tenon into a central munting?
7. Are the drawers cock-beaded (see p. 13)?
8. Do the marks on the underside of the drawers correspond with those on the dust boards over which the drawers run?

Value points

* Size has a considerable bearing on price: the smaller the chest, the more desirable, and thus the more expensive it is. This example is an ideal size.
* Some 19thC chests, in particular those made after c.1820, are very large. Many of these were virtually mass-produced and were cheaply made, with clumsy turned bun feet. These are not highly sought-after and can still be purchased for a modest amount. However, as prices for the best examples are becoming prohibitively high, middle range pieces such as that shown on the following page have begun to appreciate in value.

Bow-fronted chests

Bow-fronted chests were very fashionable between the late 18th and early 19thC. The large examples, intended for use in bedrooms, were made in quantity well into the 19thC.

Quality

Quality varies considerably. The chest on the previous page has several desirable features apart from its small size:
* thin, elegant top
* brushing slide
* well-matched veneers
* original handles
* well-shaped apron
* cock-beading around drawers
* mahogany-lined drawers.

Drawers

The base boards of the drawers run from side to side and tenon into a central munting – a feature introduced in the late 18thC to provide extra strength.

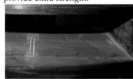

Construction

The grooves inside the carcass, *above*, were caused by the nails scraping the surface as the original munting wore down.

Back and underside

Typically, the back and underside of 19thC chests are finished with pine boards and left unpolished. Here, they have been treated with red ochre to preserve the pine. The blocks visible around the edges of the underside are for extra strengthening.

Feet

The feet of the chest are original and exhibit the usual kinds of wear. The supporting blocks behind them are, typically, in a secondary timber (pine), which has gradually rotted and pitted over the years.

Handles

The handles are original – there are no marks on the drawer front to suggest they are replacements – and, pleasingly, retain some of their gilt lacquer.

Lesser quality chest

This large (ht $44^{1}/_{2}$in/112cm) mahogany chest is of the type made in huge numbers during the 19thC. Although pleasing in its general style and proportions, it is not of the best quality and consequently has not survived in as good a condition as many finer examples.

A Swedish Beidermeier birchwood chest
c.1820; ht 36in/91.5cm; wdth 32^{1}/2in/82.5cm; value range E-F

Identification checklist for Biedermeier chests
1. Is the main wood pale, perhaps contrasted with darker mouldings?
2. Is the basic form traditional?
3. Is the veneer the main decorative feature?
4. Are the drawers without handles?
5. Are the dovetails of the drawers relatively chunky for the period?
6. Are the escutcheons of shield or lozenge shape and in a contrasting colour to the main wood?

Biedermeier furniture
Biedermeier furniture, that is, furniture made in Germany, Austria and parts of Scandinavia during the 1820s and 30s, is very popular now – and relatively inexpensive compared with other pale wood furniture of the period, such as those pieces made in satinwood in England at around the same time. It was made for a relatively mass market and this is at times reflected in the quality of construction – for example, the chest shown, *above*, has a very simple form and no attempt has been made to match up the veneers.

Woods
Blond woods, such as ash, maple, and cherrywood were preferred. The chest *above* is in birchwood – a pale wood which has a fine even grain. Fruitwoods were also very popular in the period, and, in Austria and Germany, mahogany as well, sometimes combined with blond wood. Fruitwood tends to be used on less sophisticated pieces. In Scandinavia masur birch, similar to burr, was also used.
* French furniture of the period (see facing page) is more likely to use a finer wood than birch, such as maple, which is more varied in tone and more highly figured.

Biedermeier chests

Styles vary slightly according to where the piece was made – for example, the chest shown in the main picture is typically Scandinavian in its use of a basically traditional, almost 18thC form, combined with a few details from its own period, such as the feet. Austrian and German Biedermeier tends to be sophisticated and elaborate: Scandinavian forms are simple and relatively austere.

The Scandinavian chest is of a type originally made in large quantities and still quite readily available today for relatively affordable amounts. It has several typical features:
* it is made without mouldings. The edges of this example are squared off, but examples with rounded edges are equally common
* simplicity: the furniture tended to be made for the smaller city properties rather than for grand dwellings
* use of dark contrasting mouldings
* inlaid shield-shape escutcheons
* Continental lock
* Scandinavian pine carcass – a dense wood, Scandinavian pine was readily available in the north
* lack of surface decoration, such as carving.

Drawer linings

The drawer linings are in pitch pine and are relatively chunky compared with English linings (see p. 13). The dovetails are correspondingly chunkier – a sign of the chest's provincial origins.

Escutcheons

The lonzenge-shaped escutcheon was a popular alternative to the shield form. Both types are usually in a colour that contrasts with the main wood.

Feet

The tapered foot, *above left*, is a hangover from Louis XVI styles and is not as typical as the scrolled type, *above right*.

Swedish Biedermeier

Many of the better chests were divided visually into sections, as the Swedish birchwood example, *above*, is. Other features that lift it above the ordinary include:
* chequered frieze below the top
* inlay to the top drawer
* ebonized columns flanking the central drawers
* stencil work (a little crudely executed) to the bottom drawer.

French Empire chests

The early 19thC French chest, *above*, is similar in concept to the Biedermeier pieces shown here but is more sophisticated: it has a marble top, columns headed by ormolu capitals, cast and gilded handles and applied moulding to the feet and base. The veneers are highly burred. Such a piece would also have fine dovetails and be generally well finished.

WELLINGTON CHESTS

*A 19thC English mahogany Wellington chest
c.1840; ht 45 3/4in/116cm, wdth 26in/67cm, value range D-F*

Identification checklist for 19thC Wellington chests
1. Is the chest of reddish figured mahogany, or veneered walnut?
2. Are the drawers finely dovetailed?
3. Does the chest have the characteristic locking mechanism (see facing page)?
4. Is it veneered onto a pine carcass?
5. Are the handles original?
6. Is the back unfinished?
7. Do the drawers match each other in style of construction and wood used?

Recognition point
The nulled moulding below the top of the chest shown *above* is typical of the late 1820s; it was popular into the mid-19thC.

Wellington chests
Wellington chests were first seen during the 1820s and are identified by their tall narrow shape. They are most commonly found in mahogany, often of a reddish colour and figured, but were made in a variety of other woods, such as maple and sycamore, and, in the Victorian period, veneered walnut. The decoration tends to be minimal, although walnut examples often have some inlay. They are not easily given to being altered or converted, and fakes are not known to have been made. Wellington chests were also made on the Continent of Europe (see facing page).

Drawers

The wooden knobs are the original ones: the front of the drawer shows no sign of any other handle having been there, and the back is undisturbed apart from the single nut holding the original knob in place. Many Wellington chests have had their original knobs or handles replaced with 20thC brass knobs.
* The drawers are lined in mahogany, which, from the beginning of the 19thC, began to be used more often for linings. Wellington chests often have drawer stops to prevent the drawer from falling out when opened.
* The drawers of Wellington chests are usually of equal depth, rather than graduated as in other chests. An alternative arrangement might include a secretaire drawer at an appropriate height in place of two drawers (see *below*).

Locks

English Wellington chests have a single locking mechanism, situated on a flap to the sides of the drawers, *above*, which locks in place over the edges of the drawers to prevent them from opening.
* The locks of Continental tall chests are in the centre of each drawer, as on chests and other case furniture (see *right*).

Size

Wellington chests were made in a variety of sizes – some of them are quite miniature, and useful for holding jewelry, sewing materials and so on. The example shown in the main picture is among the largest. However, unlike many other pieces of furniture, size is not an important factor in the price of these pieces: value is governed by factors such as the quality of the construction and veneers, the decorative details, and whether the piece is in good condition.

French Wellington chests

This attractive Louis-Philippe Wellington, or *semanier*, one of a pair made c.1850 in the Louis XV style, has a fall-front secretaire disguised as three top drawers. It has several typically French characteristics:
* applied ormolu mounts, cast handles, escutcheons and drawer mouldings
* marbled top.

SEAT FURNITURE

Early seat furniture is very basic and is limited to oak joined stools (pp. 50-1), and settles – a type of bench or coffer with a panelled back and arms at each end. The first chairs are of joined construction (see p. 12) and have wooden seats.

By the 17thC chairs were made in walnut as well as oak; they are often elaborately turned and carved and occasionally incorporate inlaid marquetry decoration. Chairs of this period are assessed by their originality, patina and colour. It is likely that many of them will have some replaced parts.

Chairs of the Carolean period are usually in walnut, with barley-twist supports, a caned seat and tall back. Currently, they are unfashionable and comparatively inexpensive.

From the second half of the 17thC a greater emphasis is placed on fringing. Woven cane chairs date from the 1660s, and the first really comfortable chair, the upholstered wing chair, was also introduced in the late 17thC. This was upholstered with needlework, silk velvet or silk damask although examples with original upholstery are exceptionally rare today. The wing chair continued to be popular in England and the United States throughout the Chippendale period, until the last quarter of the 18thC. Proportions vary considerably – the best examples are curvaceous, with a generous sweep to the arms and wings.

The cabriole leg dominated the early 18thC. This period also saw the introduction of the chair-back settee, an elongated seat comprising two, three or more chair backs joined together, with an arm at each end, and a single seat.

Mid-18thC styles were dominated by the leading cabinet-makers, such as George Hepplewhite and Thomas Sheraton, whose design books had a great influence on English and American furniture. By this time sofas were more in evidence; they were generally low-backed with a deep seat and sumptuous upholstery. Later in the century styles became lighter; the French influence was evident on high-fashion pieces.

The sabre leg is associated with the Regency period, when chairs were usually mahogany or rosewood and of ornate design. French Empire furniture continued to be an important influence, especially on American chairs.

Victorian designs were sturdier and more ornate. The Edwardians returned to the elegance of the late 18thC, although proportions tended to be slightly narrower and designs were, if anything, too finely drawn.

Sets of eight or more chairs, including two elbow, or armchairs, have become increasingly sought-after in the last twenty years and today command a premium; sets of four or six are more modestly priced. Each member of a set should be examined carefully: sets have sometimes been completed by taking some chairs apart and replacing one or two parts of each chair with new members, using the replaced parts to make up an extra chair, a practice known as "scrambling".

Until the end of the 17thC chairs were joined and held

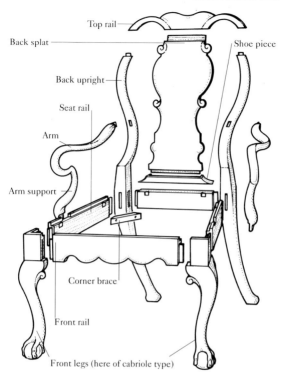

Top rail

Back splat

Shoe piece

Back upright

Seat rail

Arm

Arm support

Corner brace

Front rail

Front legs (here of cabriole type)

together by pegged tenons. The chair illustrated with its joints dissociated represents an early 18thC English chair. Quality chairs have been made in this way ever since. The joints are glued and screws help to secure the arms. In time, these joints "dry out" and the chair can become rickety. However, it is a straightforward job to "knock apart" and reassemble the chair provided animal glue has been used (never use modern super-glues – they are insoluble).

The chair drawn here is designed to take a "drop-in" or "slip-in" seat. The separate seat frame is traditionally made in beech, a strong wood which does not split when tacked for upholstery. Alternatively, the chair may have stuff-over upholstery in which the seat extends over, and thus covers, the seat rail. The older the chair, the more times it is likely to have been upholstered and the more holes there will be in the framework. Any reupholstery should be carried out using traditional materials such as horse-hair padding and tacks (rather than staples).

With any chair it is a good idea to stand back and assess its proportions – some chairs are not at all well-proportioned. A good chair will "stand well" when looked at from all angles.

Finally, sit in the chair to make sure that it is comfortable as well as good looking.

JOINED STOOLS

A mid-17thC English oak joined stool
c. 1640; ht 20in/51cm; value range D-F

Identification checklist for 17thC joined stools
1. Is the stool oak and of joined construction?
2. Are the legs simply moulded, according to the styles of the period (see pp. 110-13)?
3. Is the carving in a relatively free style, with burnished highlights?
4. Are the undersides of the top and stretchers roughly finished, and unpolished?
5. Is the top roughly hewn?
6. Do the feet exhibit the expected signs of wear?
7. Are the pegs hand-made (see Pegging)?
8. Are the peg holes in line with the side rails?
9. Does the timber of the component parts correspond in texture, grain and colour?
10. Is the frieze carved or simply moulded?
11. Are the stretchers quite plain?

Sign of quality
The stool *above* is carved all the way round; a less desirable type might be simply moulded, with no carving.

Joined stools

Joined stools, like most English
furniture of the 16th and 17thC,
were nearly always made in oak.
Originally in sets, even pairs are
very scarce now, especially in
undisturbed condition, when they
command a premium: they rarely
survive untouched the effects of
damp floors, woodworm and ill
usage.

Authentication

Beware of repairs and alterations,
especially of a replaced or re-
made top. The underside of a
genuine top will have a dry,
undisturbed appearance, and will
appear darker and slightly
patinated on the edge that
extends over the rails – the result
of absorbing the natural oils of the
hand when moved.
* Early oak that retains its original
surface can have a crusty feel.
This is a sign of genuine age,
which is difficult to reproduce
artificially.
* The feet should show
appropriate signs of age: they may
be pitted and worn away in parts;
but be suspicious of feet that look
exaggeratedly worn.

Pegging

As well as confirming that the
timber corresponds on all parts,
that patination is as described
above and that any carving
appears contemporary (see p. 14),
the best way to detect a fake or
"wrong" joined stool is to
examine the type and
arrangement of the pegs used to
secure the top to the base. Hand-
made pegs, which are irregular in
shape and stand slightly proud of
the surface, will have acquired a
degree of patination. On a
genuine piece they will be
positioned in any of the ways
shown, *above:* there should not be
any plugged holes where the top
might once have been secured to
another base. The holes should be
in line with the side rails.

Reproductions

The joined stool *above* is a
Victorian reproduction in the
17thC manner. It was not made to
deceive but over the years has
developed characteristics
associated with age which may
deceive the unwary – for example,
signs of wear on the feet and a
build-up of dirt in the crevices.
However, the Victorians used a
pale, straw-coloured kind of oak,
stained to look dark. On this
example the original colour is
visible where the polish has worn
away. Also, oak used in the
Victorian period is straight-
grained and lacking in figure,
unlike the darker, well-figured
oak used in the 17thC. The
carving should be examined in
detail. Later carving may appear
stiff and laboured compared with
the carving of a 17thC example.
The top of a period joined stool
will be roughly hewn, whereas
one made in the Victorian period
or later will have been finished by
machine and thus have a neater
appearance. Finally, fakes and
reproductions may have
artificially produced worm holes,
which are likely to be regular and
unnaturally round.

Reproduction pegs

The detail, *above,* from the
reproduction shows that an
attempt has been made to make
the pegs look hand-made.
However, they are not convincing,
and some of them are flush with
the surface, as hand-made pegs
would not be.
* Open-twist legs are uncommon
on early joined stools.

51

WAINSCOT CHAIRS

*A late 17thC English elm wainscot chair
c.1685; ht 43in/110.5cm; value range D-F*

Identification checklist for 17thC wainscot chairs

1. Is the chair oak, or, less commonly, elm?
2. Has it been made using the joined method of construction (see p. 12)?
3. Are the pegs hand-made?
4. Is any carving free in style, with burnished highlights?
5. Are any cresting rail and ear pieces original to the chair (see facing page)?
6. Do the feet show appropriate signs of wear?
7. Is the front seat rail worn where feet have rested on it over the years?
8. Is the chair well-patinated, with a build-up of dirt and wax in the inaccessible angles and crevices of the carving?
9. Do the undersides of the stretchers and the seat look dry and untouched?
10. Do the colour and timber suggest the chair is period, rather than one of the many 19thC copies?

Value point

Wainscot chairs have recently risen greatly in value. This is partly due to the revival in popularity of oak, the wood from which many of them are made.

Variations

The place of origin can usually be determined by regional features, such as carved motifs. The chair, *above*, is typical of North Yorkshire, and of country chairs generally.

The back rail
The back rail at the base has been strengthened. This is not detrimental to value although some collectors might prefer to remove the strengthening bar. The feet show the expected signs of wear.

Comfort
The rake, or angled back, *above, left*, for added comfort, is a desirable feature and compares favourably with the rigidly upright back of the oak chair shown *below* and in profile *above right*.

Shrinkage
There is some shrinkage in the boards of the seat – the natural result of age. The wood beneath the seat is dry and untouched.

Cresting rails and ear pieces
These can be replaced, or added to a plain chair at a later date. As the cresting rail is made separately from the chair back, there will be a joint even if the rail is original to the chair (see detail *above*), as it is in the example on p.52. However, the patina of the rail should match that of the rest of the chair. A few flamboyant chairs were designed without ear pieces but with elaborate cresting rails overhanging, and curving toward, the sides of the chair. Cresting rails designed to accompany ear pieces will extend beyond the frame of the chair but will not curve in toward it.

Lesser quality wainscot chair
This oak chair is also late-17thC. However, it has a replaced seat and one replaced side stretcher. It is also countryfied in design, with an upright back and no rake (see *above*). The single lozenge motif is very common, and as the chair's sole decoration is somewhat uninspiring. Value is seriously reduced by the fact that the seat is a replacement, even though it was made using 17thC wood. The replaced seat and side stretcher are easily detected through inconsistencies in the grain and patina of the wood. The arms and back are noticeably richer in colour than the replaced parts, and, unlike the rest of the chair, the seat is coarse-grained. A less serious, but significant factor, is the degree of wear on the blocks of the feet, which have worn down to the tenons.

A late 17thC Dutch walnut armchair
c.1685-90; ht 51in/129.5cm; value range E-F

Identification checklist for late 17thC armchairs
1. Is the chair walnut?
2. Is it of joined construction (see p. 12)?
3. Are the pegs hand-made (irregular in shape and standing slightly proud of the surface)?
4. Is the chair back very high (up to approx. 55in/140cm)?
5. Are the seat and back caned?
6. Is the front stretcher highly carved or ornately turned?
7. Is the carving bold, and fairly free?
8. Does the chair have scroll feet?
9. Does it have an H-shaped stretcher (for extra strength) or a flat, ornately carved stretcher?

Value point
These chairs often come in pairs. A pair is worth significantly more than two single chairs.

Walnut

Although oak was the main wood for much late 17thC provincial English and Dutch furniture, this type of chair was usually made of walnut, a softer wood that lends itself well to turning and carving – forms of decoration favoured by the Dutch during the 17thC. Walnut was also used extensively from Charles II's reign for more sophisticated pieces. Because walnut is prone to worm, many of these chairs are in poor condition, and should be carefully examined for signs of weakness (see *below* and *right*).

Cane

Cane was first seen on English chairs after c.1660, both for the seats and in back panels. By c.1685 canework had become finer and the holes more regular. Although it is preferable to have the original cane, replacements are acceptable. New cane is very pale and can take a long time to mellow. Cane was popular again in the late 18thC and Regency.

Reproductions

Chairs (and other furniture) of this period were reproduced in the Victorian period, generally in oak, and artificially stained to an almost black colour that gives them a distinctly Victorian look. They are not likely to be confused with the originals as they lack the usual signs of wear and the pegged construction.

Variations

The same rules of examination apply to upholstered versions as for those without upholstery. Examples with original upholstery are now very rare.

Condition

Being tall and of relatively soft wood, these chairs can be unstable. This one has been reinforced somewhat unskilfully at the back with a rather obvious reinforcing block, which reduces the value of the chair. However, it is easily removed and careful restoration can cure the problem.

English or Continental?

Although this chair is Dutch, it is very similar to those made in England at the same period or slightly later. The tell-tale sign of a Continental chair is the fact that the turning of the stretcher tenons directly into the leg, as in the detail *above*, whereas on English chairs any stretchers end in square blocks. American chairs tend to follow the Continental style.
* The canework may also provide a clue to origin: oval panels are usually Dutch, whereas English panels are rectangular.

Back legs

The back legs of the chair have been built up slightly. This is acceptable on a piece of this age, provided that the restoration is not extensive and has been properly done. Metal plates have been applied to the front feet, which had been weakened by rot – a somewhat amateurish form of repair.

Woodworm

The walnut versions of these chairs are prone to woodworm. Although evident in this chair, it is not excessive.

LADDER- AND SPINDLE-BACK CHAIRS

An English ash ladder-back chair
Late 18th/early 19thC; ht 44in/118cm; value range C-D

Identification checklist for 18th and 19thC ladder- and spindle-back chairs.
1. Is the chair ash (the turner's favourite material)?
2. On ladder-backs, are the horizontal members wavy?
3. Does the chair have a rush seat?
4. Are the legs turned?
5. Does the chair have an ornately turned front stretcher, with plain stretchers at the sides and back?
6. Are the splats or spindles original?

Ladder- and spindle-back chairs

Ladder-back chairs were made from the 1760s until well into the 19thC. Many come from Lancashire or Yorkshire. The shape of the ladders and of the top rail help to identify their origin. Another variety is the type with a spindle back (see *facing page*), also made in the provinces, especially in Cheshire.

Collecting

Spindle-back chairs are more common than ladder-backs, and are inexpensive singly, although carvers fetch more than chairs without arms. Ladder-backs are generally the more popular and thus more expensive type, perhaps because the shaped ladders provide a greater degree of comfort than the more upright spindles.

Matched sets

Sets are becoming increasingly scarce. Collectors should note that these chairs were not made up as formal sets, but were matched, either at the time of making or subsequently, and this, together with the fact that they are all hand-made, means that minor variations are inevitable. It is likely that among a set of eight at least one chair will be a later example, so all parts of all chairs should be thoroughly examined.

Reproductions

To be regarded as period, ladder- and spindle-back chairs should have been made before the 1830s. Reproductions were made during the early 20thC. Period examples can usually be identified by the wear on the feet and stretchers, and by the patination on the arms and top rail, parts of which will have faded to a nice golden colour. Early 20thC reproductions are often made in a blander wood or may be artificially stained to give an appearance of age.

Condition

Examine the following areas:
* Rungs: on chairs with ladder-backs, one or more "rungs" may be replacements. Close inspection will reveal any timber that does not match the rest of the chair.
* Stretchers: these are simply glued and tenoned into the leg, and sometimes become loose and and drop off. Check for discrepancies in the wood. Replacements of the plain side rails are acceptable but chairs with replaced turned rails suffer a loss in value.
* Seats: these are made of rush, which is then faced with a wooden strip. Modern rush is completely acceptable.
* Feet: these may be in need of building up if the chair has been reduced in height, perhaps to remove rot. They may already have been spliced and built up, in which case there will be a visible joint low down on the leg. Such a repair to a back leg is not as detrimental as to a front one.

Spindle-backs

Spindles are particularly fragile and are often replaced: compare the colour of the wood and the grain direction of each spindle of each chair. Older spindle-backs have finial tops similar to those found on ladder-back chairs (see main picture). Spindle-back chairs with arms (*above left*) are usually in three tiers; examples without arms (*above right*) have two tiers.
* Both spindle- and ladder-back chairs are popularly used with oak refectory tables as it is virtually impossible to find sets of 17thC chairs today.

WINDSOR CHAIRS

An early 19thC English Windsor chair
c.1810; ht 35in/89cm, wdth 21in/53.5cm; value code F

Identification checklist for early 19thC Windsor chairs
1. Are the supports, splat, front legs and bow in yew, elm or ash?
2. Does the chair have a saddle-shaped ash or elm seat?
3. Does it have a crinoline ("cowhorn") or H-shaped stretcher or, occasionally in the United States, a stretcher uniting each pair of legs?
4. Are the back legs in a secondary wood, probably beech or ash?
5. Are the spindles yew, or in a secondary wood?
6. Does the chair look undisturbed at the joints?
7. Does it have a central shaped splat with pierced decoration?

Replaced splats and spindles
Replacements seriously reduce value. As well as being in wood of a different colour and type from the rest of the chair, they will lack the shading that usually builds up in the crevices and around the joints – for example, where the spindles meet the seat and arms. The joints may look disturbed where the new splat or spindles have been fitted.

Windsor chairs

Windsor chairs, the most popular and recognizable type of English provincial chair, were made occasionally during the second half of the 18thC but predominantly between 1800 and 1840. The backs are usually composed of straight "sticks", sometimes with a central decorative splat, and more rarely, with alternate plain straight sticks and more decorative ones.

Value

There are two main forms: high and low back. The example, *left,* is of the low-back type. High back Windsors may fetch in the region of 25 per cent more than low backs. Yew wood Windsors are generally worth 30% or 40% more than elm examples. Windsor chairs with arms are usually found singly; pairs command a premium. * A central splat adds to the price.

Wheelbacks

Windsor chairs with a wheelback splat, like that shown *above*, are the best known type in England. The hoop-shaped top is typically English.

Reproductions

A great many reproductions were made in the 1920s and 30s and are of insignificant value. They are in poorer quality timber and although they will have some signs of age, these will be less pronounced than on a period chair. In particular, the edges of the uprights and the highlights will be sharper and the colour not as mellow.

American Windsor chairs

American Windsors, made in the second half of the 18th and early part of the 19thC, differ in a number of details from English versions, especially in not usually having a central decorative splat. The New England Windsor chair has a small writing shelf. The more spindles it has, the older and more desirable the chair is considered to be. There are many regional variations.

Mid-18thC styles

This "comb-back" Windsor chair from c.1765 has a characteristic American form, especially in its addition of a top rail. The scrolling at the end of the arms was a feature of American Chippendale-period chairs.

Early 19thC styles

Many American Windsors, such as this one from c.1800/10, have splayed legs set well into the seat, which gives them a more angled appearance than the legs on English Windsor chairs. The squared top and the stretcher uniting the back legs are also peculiarly American.

CABRIOLE-LEG CHAIRS

An early 18thc English walnut cabriole-leg side chair
c.1720-25; ht 42in/106cm; value range D-F

Identification checklist for early 18thC cabriole-leg chairs
1. Is the chair walnut or oak? (Mahogany was usual from the 1740s, except on provincial pieces.)
2. Is it fairly simple in outline?
3. Is the splat a relatively restrained vase-shape, and fairly upright?
4. If the knees of the legs are carved, do they have shell motifs?
5. If the back legs are not cabrioles, are they square and flaring outwards?
6. Has the chair been tenoned and glued (rather than pegged)?
7. Does it have a drop-in seat?
8. Does it have a shoe piece (see p. 67)?

High quality or provincial?
The chair shown *above* is a standard provincial example of nice but not exceptional quality. It is in solid timber throughout (apart from the splat, which is veneered onto oak). A more sophisticated example would probably have a veneered back splat, uprights and seat rails on a walnut base, giving a more

decorative effect than can be achieved with solid timber. Such chairs would also have carving on the knees of the legs. Chairs that retain stretchers at this date are likely to be of provincial origin – in the major cabinet-making areas chairs were now sufficiently strong in design and construction not to need the added support afforded by stretchers.

Cabriole-leg chairs
The fully developed cabriole-leg came to prominence during the reign of Queen Anne, and is found on English and American chairs and other furniture throughout the first half of the 18thC (and for much of the second half, but with a French influence). In the early 18thC it is associated with a pad foot, but more ornate feet were also used.

Seats
18thC seats are of the drop-in or stuff-over upholstered type. From the Queen Anne period the drop-in seat simply sits within the seat framework, as this one does.
* The seat rail should be examined carefully: if drop-in seats are overstuffed and pushed hard onto the frame, they may put pressure on the rail joints, causing them to split.

Splats
Vase-shaped splats are typical of the early 18thC, and in contrast to splats of the Chippendale period, are invariably unpierced. This one is veneered in walnut onto oak, rather than walnut, which is indicative of provincial manufacture. The figuring of the veneer is quite plain. The splats of early 18thC chairs follow the shape of the sitter's back.

Reproductions
This c.1900 Queen Anne-style walnut dining chair incorporates all the best Queen Anne features:
* carved cabrioles
* scrollwork on ear pieces
* shell-shaped drop-in seat
* curvaceous splat
* veneered back and seat rail
* back as well as front cabrioles
It can be identified as 19thC by a certain stiffness of design in the splat and the cabrioles, which lack the fullness of the early 18thC ones. The lack of a shoe piece is also characteristic of 19thC construction. The chair does not display the kind of wear usually found on earlier examples. However, as reproductions, rather than fakes, these chairs are now highly collectable in their own right.

Construction
By the early 18thC most chairs were tenoned and glued rather than pegged, as this one is. The strengthening dowels were added at a later date.
* The dark shading in the corners and angles is a sign of age.

WING CHAIRS

*An Irish Queen Anne-period wahut wing armchair
c.1710; ht 47in/119cm; wdth 34in/88cm; value range B-E.*

Identification checklist for Queen Anne-period wing chairs

1. Is the chair walnut?
2. Does it have cabriole legs?
3. Is it constructed without stretchers?
4. Is it well-shaped, with nicely scrolled arms?
5. Is the frame, including the underside, original?
6. Are the ear pieces original (see p. 90)?

Value point
Most examples have two front cabriole legs and two square legs at the back. The type with four cabrioles is generally more desirable.

Wing chairs
These comfortable upholstered armchairs were introduced in England after the Restoration, and in the United States from c.1700. The cabriole leg, first seen in the late 17thC, was fully developed by the early 18thC – the period of the classic Queen Anne walnut wing chair *above*. The most obvious differences between this type and the rather ornate styles of the 17thC wing chairs, with their busily carved legs and stretchers, are the lack of stretchers, and the simple elegance of the cabriole leg. Wing chairs continued to be made well into the Chippendale period – when they usually had square legs, either with or without carving – and provincially throughout the second half of the 18thC.

62

Ear pieces

From the underside it is also possible to examine the ear pieces on the inside of the legs, at the top. At least some of these should be original (see p. 90). Minor splits in original ear pieces are to be expected.

Reupholstery

Dealers and collectors will often have chairs reupholstered as long as they are structurally sound. In such a case it may be difficult to check whether the frame beneath the upholstery is original, although it may be possible to tell by examining the seat from the underside (see p. 77). However, many dealers keep pictures of the chair before the work was carried out. The chair shown *opposite* is pictured *above* before being reupholstered.

* It is preferable to have chairs reupholstered in a material that is in keeping with the original type and style. The material used for this chair is hand-woven, hand-coloured silk made in Lyon using 18thC techniques.

Legs and feet

The hairy cusps at the back of the feet, and the sunflowers on the knees of the leg (in addition to the more typical harebells), suggest an Irish provenance. Similar details are also found on some Colonial chairs of this period or a little later. The carving is intaglio-carved on a pounce background, rather than cameo-carved which is the more usual method. An especially good feature is the almost exaggerated shape of the back legs – the alternative would be a fairly plain square swept back leg with chamfered edges.

* Check that that each leg and foot is original: new wood is sometimes spliced in between a foot and a leg when making a repair. Occasionally, the lower part of a leg is replaced altogether.

Condition

This detail of the framework shows that the chair was fundamentally sound before work was carried out. There are no splits in the wood, and only a small amount of inactive woodworm. The holes around the outer edges show where the original upholstery was attached.

CHIPPENDALE CHAIRS

*An English Chippendale-period mahogany dining chair
c.1765; ht 36in/91.5cm; wdth 20in/52cm; value range C-E.*

Identification checklist for Chippendale chairs
1. Is the chair mahogany?
2. Is it carved?
3. Does it have square chamfered legs united by fairly
plain stretchers?
4. If a set, do all the chairs match in type of wood and
style of construction?
5. Are the seat rails original? (See Seats *opposite*.)
6. Does the chair have a shoe piece (see facing page)?
7. Is the chair well-proportioned (a key factor with this
type of chair)?
8. Is the seat either of the drop-in or stuff-over type (see
p. 49).

Condition
Chairs are particularly prone to
the effects of wear and tear,
although the one shown *above* is
in a remarkably good state of
preservation. If there is damage, it
will probably be to the top of the
uprights by the top rail, and in the
64

seat area, where the timber
receives a lot of strain.
Reupholstery is almost inevitable.
The beech seat rails may show
signs of worm. This is not serious
as long as the worm is inactive
and has not structurally weakened
the timber (see p. 17).

Thomas Chippendale

The most famous and skilled of England's master cabinet-makers, Thomas Chippendale had an enormous impact on furniture-making in the 18thC. His *Gentleman and Cabinet Maker's Director* of 1762 was used by most English furniture makers as the basis of their designs; thus many so-called Chippendale chairs were not made by Chippendale himself, or at his workshop, but were copies of styles he produced or illustrated in his *Director.* Unless it is documented, it can be difficult to prove that a particular piece came from Chippendale's own workshops, as his work was unsigned. The chair on the previous page is typical of the Chippendale style, especially in its Gothic-type splat. The carved top rail and good nutty brown colour are particularly fine. There is a huge variety of Chippendale-style chairs, but the general outline of this example is typical.

Shoe pieces

Collectors should always take as many factors into account as possible, as perfectly "right" pieces occasionally have untypical features – for example, on chairs of the Chippendale period the back splat usually slots into a shoe piece (a narrow plain section between the back seat rail and the splat, see p. 48); in this example, the splat tenons directly into the seat rail, but the chair is genuine.

Seats

Seats may be of the drop-in upholstered type, or stuff-over. This example is stuff-over, and has been reupholstered (see p. 63). If the reupholstery covers the framework of the chair, turn the chair upside down and examine the seat rails; if they are original they will have a dry look (which occurs when wood is not handled or polished), and there should be no signs of newly cut wood or regular edges that have not had time to become rounded with wear.

Uprights and top rail

The good intricate carving of the shaped top rail is a particularly desirable feature that enhances the value. Most sets of Chippendale chairs found today will have plainer top rails than this one (but see **Reproductions** *below*). Breaks sometimes occur in the scrolled ends of top rails and at the top of uprights, and a joint or other repair would be impossible to disguise against close inspection.

Reproductions

Chippendale-style chairs were often copied in the Victorian period and the copies are now very collectable in their own right. The chair, *above*, is one of a typical set of eight. Although it is mahogany, and is numbered, as many chairs made during the Chippendale period are, it can be distinguished from chairs made during the Chippendale period through the following features:
* the use of several Chippendale-style elements exaggerated and crammed into a single item – for example, the cabriole legs are very pronounced; the base of the splat is over-elaborate, and there is a large amount of carving
* the quality of the carving, which, though competent, is rather stiff and lifeless. It is also shallower than 18thC carving, with less undercutting
* the timber, which lacks a degree of warmth and patina
* the lack of a shoe piece
* a lesser degree of wear than the period examples
* the use of corner brackets, which were not found on chairs until the 19thC.

CORNER CHAIRS

A mid-18thC English mahogany corner, or writing, chair c.1745/50; ht 32in/82.5cm; value code F

Identification checklist for 18thC corner chairs
1. Is the chair either mahogany or Virginia walnut?
2. Does it have a vase-shaped splat, perhaps with pierced decoration?
3. Does the chair have the characteristic Chippendale cabrioles or chamfered square legs?
4. Is the seat of the drop-in type?
5. Is the construction fairly solid, and bold?
6. If the chair has stretchers, are they plain?
7. Do the lower legs and feet exhibit the expected signs of wear?
7. Are the seat rails in the primary wood?

Corner chairs
Corner chairs were popular in England during the first half of the 18thC. They are usually found singly. The example, *above*, is relatively plain, but has some good features – for example, a well-profiled splat with pierced detail. The most expensive type, from the Queen Anne period, is walnut with veneered seat rails and splat, cabriole legs and some carved decoration, often a shell

motif. Other good examples are also found in mahogany or · Virginia walnut. More basic corner chairs are in oak and other country woods, such as elm, and have straight legs and no carving. Corner chairs (and their variants, see opposite page) continued to be made provincially during the second half of the 18thC. They were very popular in the United States, in styles similar to their English counterparts.

Shoe pieces
The chair has a shoe piece, or slipper section, between the back splat and the seat rail. In 18thC chairs the slipper section was made separately, as it is here, whereas 19thC chair backs are made in one piece. Later, 19thC examples can also be identified by:
* their relative fussiness, often with light intricate inlaid decoration, which is not a feature of 18thC corner chairs
* their even colour: earlier chairs have a good, varied surface, being made from a rich mahogany, parts of which will have received more exposure to light.

Corner brackets
Corner brackets are usually in a secondary wood and unpolished, as these are, and should resemble the other unpolished areas of the chair. However, these brackets look new and may be replacements or later additions. As a genuine repair, this will not reduce the value of the chair.

Condition
The chair has a fine colour and patina, and is in good original condition although there are one or two splits in the top rail. The arm is nicely shaped, as is the back rail. The chair exhibits some signs of age, especially at the front leg toward the foot. The moulding at the front, crisp at the top, has all but disappeared lower down. There are small chunks missing from the back feet, but this will not seriously reduce the value.

Legs
Square legs, chamfered at the back, like those of the chair on p. 66, are characteristic of the Chippendale period. The more sought-after and expensive alternative is the type with cabrioles (see *below*), either carved or plain. Some chairs have one cabriole leg at the front and plain ones at the sides and back.

George II corner chair
This good cabriole leg corner chair, made in Cuban mahogany, c.1740, is typical of George II furniture in its solidity and severe appearance. Like the straight-legged type, it also has vase-shaped splats. Note that the cabriole-leg type has no stretchers.

Commode chairs
A variant of the corner chair is the rather inelegant commode chair, which has a deep frieze below the seat rail to conceal the pot. These chairs have never been very sought-after and many have had the commode part removed. The easiest way to detect this is to examine the legs: once the deep frieze is removed or reduced in depth, filled holes will be visible where it was originally tenoned into the leg (see *below*).

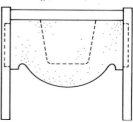

CHAIR BACKS

English

Early 16thC
bobbin frame

17thC
arcaded panel

2nd half
17thC, Yorkshire

Early 17thC
caned back

Cromwellian
padded back

Charles II
with caned panel

Late 17thC
bobbin turned

Late 17thC
slat back

2nd half
17thC

Late
17thC

William & Mary
with tall back

Early 18thC

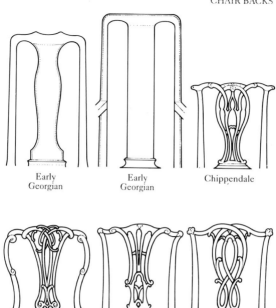

Early
Georgian

Early
Georgian

Chippendale

Chippendale

Chippendale

Chippendale

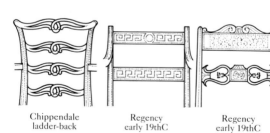

Chippendale
ladder-back

Regency
early 19thC

Regency
early 19thC

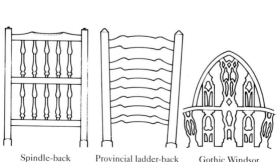

Spindle-back
1730/1830

Provincial ladder-back
1730/1830

Gothic Windsor
2nd half 18thC

Early 19thC
Windsor

Early
Victorian

Victorian

Victorian

Victorian

Victorian

Victorian

Victorian
Elizabethan

Victorian
papier mâché

Victorian
papier mâché

Victorian
button-back

Victorian

American

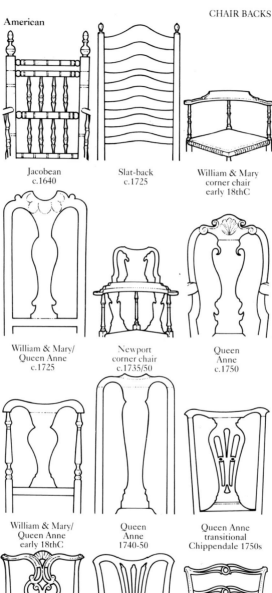

Jacobean
c.1640

Slat-back
c.1725

William & Mary
corner chair
early 18thC

William & Mary/
Queen Anne
c.1725

Newport
corner chair
c.1735/50

Queen
Anne
c.1750

William & Mary/
Queen Anne
early 18thC

Queen
Anne
1740-50

Queen Anne
transitional
Chippendale 1750s

Chippendale
1760s

Chippendale
1770-80

Chippendale
ladderback
1770-90

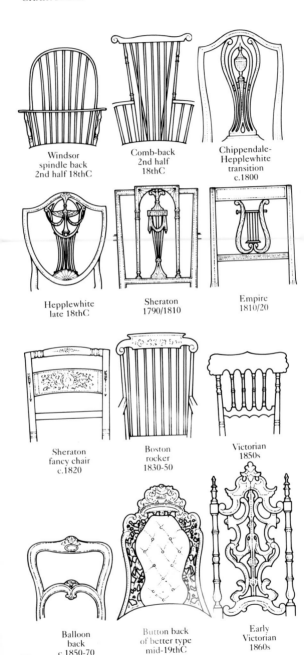

Windsor
spindle back
2nd half 18thC

Comb-back
2nd half
18thC

Chippendale-
Hepplewhite
transition
c.1800

Hepplewhite
late 18thC

Sheraton
1790/1810

Empire
1810/20

Sheraton
fancy chair
c.1820

Boston
rocker
1830-50

Victorian
1850s

Balloon
back
c.1850-70

Button back
of better type
mid-19thC

Early
Victorian
1860s

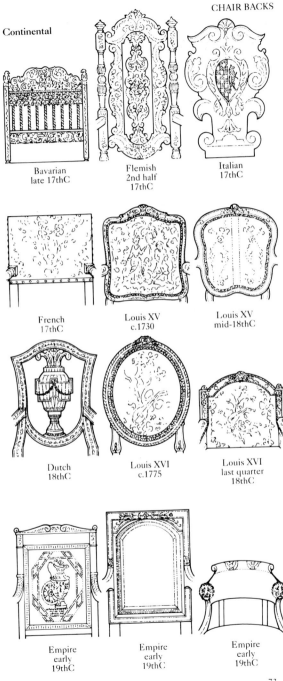

Continental

Bavarian
late 17thC

Flemish
2nd half
17thC

Italian
17thC

French
17thC

Louis XV
c.1730

Louis XV
mid-18thC

Dutch
18thC

Louis XVI
c.1775

Louis XVI
last quarter
18thC

Empire
early
19thC

Empire
early
19thC

Empire
early
19thC

73

A late 18thC English mahogany shield-back chair c.1785; ht 32in/81cm; value range E-F

Identification checklist for late 18thC chairs in the Hepplewhite style

1. Is the chair mahogany?
2. Does it have a shield-shaped back with a pierced splat?
3. Are the legs square, elegant and tapering?
4. Does the chair have "spade" feet (see p. 183)?
5. Does it have finely carved decoration?
6. Are the arms downswept?

Late 18thC chairs

In the last quarter of the 18thC chairs became lighter in style than they had been in the Chippendale period. The best-known designers of this period were Robert Adam, who introduced the square tapering leg; Thomas Hepplewhite, originator of the shield-back chair, shown above, and who also favoured oval-, heart- and lyre-shaped backs; and Thomas Sheraton, whose chairs typically had rectangular backs, with fine carved swags and other decorative details. The chair shown, *above*, originally part of a set, is a good example of a Hepplewhite period shield-back mahogany elbow chair, on elegant typical square tapering legs with spade feet. The seat is drop-in but could equally well have been stuffover.

Attribution

Unusually, the chair *opposite* bears the initials of the maker, AS, on the underside of one of the seat rails, a nice, but by no means essential feature. The chair is also numbered 11 in fairly crude punched strokes, indicating that it was originally part of a large set.
* The undersides of the stretchers and seat rails should have a dry, undisturbed look.

Adam-style chairs

Another type of English chair from the second half of the 18thC shows a strong French influence, typified by the giltwood Adamesque elbow chair, *above*, c.1765-70. In addition to its overall shape, its French-style features include:
* scrollwork arms
* oval back
* reeded legs with fluted toes
* carving at the top of the legs
* gilding.

The chair back

The chair has a number of nicely carved, crisply executed details, including leaves, central oval patera and an attractive top rail.
* Expect protruding areas, such as the centre of any paterae, to be paler in colour where they have been rubbed over the years and the polish has worn. The moulded definition on the arms of this chair has been rubbed and almost worn away – a good sign of authenticity.
* Chairs with this type of delicate design usually have some sort of repair. Small splits of the type that sometimes occur where the arm joins the top rail are not serious. However, spliced or replaced legs or stretchers will reduce the value.

Reproductions

Reproductions, made from the Victorian period, generally lack the characteristic refinement of the originals. Modern copies exist, but these will not exhibit the expected signs of wear, and they are commonly given away by their proportions, which are frequently too slender. They are made from poorer timber and are thus paler than the 18thC originals.

Regilding

The carving of the Adamesque chair shown at the top of this page is crisp and well-defined, and regilding has restored the pleasant, lively finish the chair would originally have had. Regilding, whether of parts or of an entire piece, is not detrimental to value provided that the work has been properly done, as it has been here: the chair has been water-gilded, as it would have been in the 18thC, to produce a lively finish with burnished highlights.
* Oil gilding is an alternative, less expensive method of gilding, more suitable to small expanses and where a more uniform appearance is required.

SABRE-LEG CHAIRS

An English Regency-period mahogany sabre-leg elbow chair c.1810; ht 32in/81cm; value range D-F

Identification checklist for Regency sabre-leg chairs
1. Is the chair mahogany (or rosewood)?
2. Is it constructed without stretchers?
3. Is there a pronounced curve to the front legs?
4. Are the arms heavily scrolled, and supported by the side rails?
5. Does the chair have a drop-in seat?
6. Does the seat rail exhibit the expected signs of wear?

Recognition points
* From the 1780s Regency chairs with the type of back shown, *above*, were also made with turned legs, which became increasingly bolder during the period.
* Early 19thC sabre-leg chairs are often decorated with carved scrolling formal leaves and, on the top rail, carved tulips.

Signs of quality
This chair has a number of desirable features, including the:
* warm, golden colour of the mahogany
* nicely carved shape of the arm
* fine timber with a good patina
* generous sweep to the sabre legs
* crisp carving.

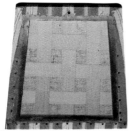

Seats

The seat of the chair in the main picture is upholstered onto a beech frame and simply drops into the chair. Other examples may have caned seats with squab cushions.
* In Regency chairs the seat sits within side rails but on top of the front rail, and is held in place with a locating lug.
* In chairs of the Chippendale period the drop-in seat usually sits within the framework.

Upholstery

Beech has been used for the seat rail as it does not split when the pins that secure the upholstery are driven in. However, it is prone to woodworm, evidence of which can be seen, *above*, in the small irregular holes in the wood. The row of larger, more regular marks near the outer edge of the rail shows where previous upholstery has been secured.
* Neither re-covering the seat with new fabric, nor reupholstering it, will adversely affect value, provided that the work has been properly done, using tacks rather than a staplegun, and horsehair stuffing in preference to foam or other synthetic materials.

Trafalgar chairs

A popular and much-copied type of sabre-leg chair was the Trafalgar chair, decorated with naval motifs, such as rope-twists or anchors, in commemoration of Nelson's victory at Trafalgar in 1805.

Reproductions

Modern sabre-leg dining chairs can usually be detected by the poorer quality of the timber, which tends to be stained a fairly tell-tale uniform colour, and the lack of signs of wear. A period mahogany chair is likely to be heavier than a reproduction.

Painted chairs

Painted furniture was extremely fashionable during the Regency period. The example, *above*, is typical, with its swags (on the legs) and lions. It retains much of its original decoration: painted furniture is often restored or completely redecorated. If the decoration is original some parts will be more worn than others – for example, on the tops of the arms where they have been rubbed. Look in the crevices around the carving for signs of paint in another colour.

Decoration

The decoration has been repolished to liven it up and to ensure that the new gilding blends in well with the original gilding.

BERGÈRE CHAIRS

*One of a pair of French Empire mahogany bergères
c.1810/20; ht 36in/91cm; value range C-E.*

Identification checklist for bergère chairs
1. Is the chair mahogany (or fruitwood)?
2. Is the style sober and restrained?
3. Does the chair have a square upholstered padded back?
4. Does it have upholstered sides with show-wood arms?
5. Does it have applied cast mouldings, and little or no carving?
6. Is the padding quite full at the back and sides?

Bergère chairs
Bergères, the French term for upholstered armchairs with a long seat, were made throughout Europe during the 18th and early 19thC. This is a typical early 19thC French example, with its sober legs and simple mouldings (in stark contrast to 18thC chair designs). Some versions have open arms. The carving, which is also restrained and relatively formal, with a slight Egyptian influence evident in the
78

palmettes, is restricted to small areas – wood carving is not usually the primary decorative element on Empire furniture; the emphasis tends to be on the applied cast mouldings. Most are mahogany, occasionally gilded. Fruitwood examples are invariably of provincial origin but, unlike some other country-made furniture, are not generally of lesser value. The square upholstered back of the example shown, *above*, is typical.

Reproductions

Bergère chairs have been continuously reproduced and are still being made today. Reproductions might include features that were not seen on the period originals, but the biggest giveaway is usually in the poorer quality of the wood.

Reupholstery

The nail marks, *above*, on the underside of the chair in the main picture were made when the webbing, instead of being attached to the seat rail as it would have been originally, was used to support the springs employed in the reupholstery – a popular but incorrect method.

19thC English-style bergère chairs

The George IV/William IV armchair, *above*, of c.1830, is of the type referred to in England as bergère. Such chairs traditionally have caned seats, back and sides, with a heavy squab seat and sometimes an upholstered back squab. They are almost invariably mahogany. This example has the characteristic scrolled arms and solidly turned legs of its period.

Fauteuils

The mid-18thC Louis XV walnut *fauteuil*, *above*, shows another classic French style. It is in polished walnut, and carved; such chairs are also found in giltwood. The style was particularly influential with English cabinet-makers during the second half of the 18thC. These chairs are also found as bergères, or with a show-wood back.
* French chairs are often stamped underneath one of the seat rails with the maker's initials.
* The fine old needlework upholstery is a very desirable feature.

Later English-style bergère chairs

The other main style of English bergère, *above*, was reproduced extensively in the 19th and early 20thC using the same methods of construction as the earlier chairs. The main way to date these chairs is to examine the quality and colour of the timber and look for signs of wear. However, collectors should bear in mind that on both the original chairs and on the reproductions, the cane and the squab seat and back are likely to be modern replacements.

BALLOON-BACK CHAIRS

A high-quality English Victorian balloon-back chair
c.1860; ht 36in/91.5cm; value range F-G

Identification checklist for 19thC balloon-back chairs
1. Is the chair walnut?
2. Is it of graceful, elegant proportions?
3. Does it have carved decoration?
4. Are the front legs French-style cabrioles with French scroll feet?
5. Does the chair have a stuff-over seat (see p. 49) with beech rails?
6. Does the chair show appropriate signs of wear – for example, on the feet?

Value points
The chair shown, *above,* has a number of desirable features that enhance its value:
* the tapestry needlework covering which, unusually, is original to the chair
* graceful and elegant shape
* crisp carving and well-formed legs.

Balloon-back chairs
These chairs were made between c.1850 and c.1880-90 and were inspired by Continental designs. Many finer examples were made as part of a suite and came in sets of four or six with a loo table. They were intended for the salon, rather than as dining chairs, so carvers are extremely rare. At their best, balloon-back chairs are light and elegant. The finer examples have cabriole front legs and are usually in walnut, although examples exist in rosewood. There are also many relatively unattractive examples made in their thousands for a mass market (see *below right*).

Fakes
Balloon-back chairs are likely to be genuine: they have not been faked because they have always been in plentiful supply and modestly priced. However, some Victorian-style chairs have recently been imported to England and the United States from the Far East. These are heavier than the Victorian originals and are obvious copies.

Construction
Typically, the top and uprights of this chair were made separately. Joints, though visible, should be subtle, as they are here.
* Check the colour and grain match of all sections to ascertain that all the parts are original. However, bear in mind that because the chair is made from separate pieces, the grain may run in different directions.

Carving
Balloon-back chairs usually have a degree of carving. On this example the carved decoration, which is well-defined, is relatively restrained.

Seat
Somewhat unusually, corner braces have been used at the front of the chair seat, and corner brackets at the back. At this period corner brackets throughout would be the more typical arrangement.

Reupholstery
The seat has been reupholstered using a staple gun instead of tacks (see p. 49). This is evident from the underside of the chair, and where the braid has come unstuck slightly, *above*.

Lesser balloon-back
This is a typical mahogany example of the heavier type of mass-produced balloon back dining chair and is of reasonable quality. The worst are of basic design, poor construction and inferior timber, and are likely to suffer from breaks and splits.

SETTEES

An English Chippendale-period mahogany settee
c.1765; ht 35³/₄in/91cm, wdth 57¹/₂in/146cm; value range D-E

Identification checklist for 18thC settees
1. Is the settee mahogany (or less commonly, giltwood)?
2. Is it upholstered onto its original, fairly crude beech framework?
3. Does it combine elegance with comfort?
4. Does the timber have a waxed finish?
5. Does the settee show signs of French influence (see below)?

18thC settees
From the mid-18thC the influence of French designs on settees (as on English furniture in general, and some American furniture) becomes quite evident. In the sofa *above* it can be seen in the shape and moulding of the cabriole leg, the French scrolled arms and toes, and the overall rococo-influenced design. Some 18thC settees sacrifice comfort to elegance, but this manages to combine the two. It is also of a desirable size: settees of this period are often too large and grandiose for the average house.

Examining the seat framework
The seat will be upholstered onto a fairly crude beech framework, which should be original: turn the settee upside down and examine the underside. The piece is likely to have been reupholstered two or three times, but the dealer may have a picture of it stripped down before the work was carried out. An original framework will show signs of the old tack holes, and probably of worm (which should be inactive, see p. 17), and may also show signs of a repair or two, as such pieces inevitably incur damage over time.

Condition and authenticity

The settee should be in basically good condition. However, certain signs of wear in addition to those on the seat framework are to be expected, and provide confirmation of authenticity:

* There will be a certain amount of shrinkage in the joints and where the ear pieces are applied.
* Prone surfaces and carving will show evidence of wear, especially along the seat rail.
* The carving will vary in tone – some areas will have been handled more or been exposed to more sunlight than other parts.
* Some of the polish may have worn away, possibly even to the actual timber, as has happened with the settee in the main picture, which shows paler in worn areas – for example, in the centre front leg and along the seat rail.
* Legs and feet are also vulnerable, especially the front ones. The undersides will show signs of wear difficult to reproduce artificially. Settees such as that shown *opposite*, with relatively slender legs, may show evidence of damage or repairs low down, toward the feet.
* Settees of any age will almost certainly have been reupholstered, preferably with webbing rather than springs (see p. 77).

Construction

A joint is visible, *above*, low down on the arm and immediately below that on the legs. This is because the settee would have been made in separate, joined sections in order to use the timber economically. The joints would not have been visible originally but will have opened up or moved slightly over time as the result of shrinkage in the wood.

Finish

English and American 18thC settees usually have a waxed surface although the trend in France and Continental Europe in general was for a high gloss polish, which tends to look a little harsh.

Chair-back settees

The chair-back type of settee, first seen during the early 18thC, was the precursor of the type with an upholstered back. They were made in walnut, mahogany or Virginia walnut, and most were of double- or triple-back form. This satinwood example is a late 19thC/Edwardian revival of a classic Sheraton design. Typically for revival furniture, it has more painted decoration than an original would have had, and the rendering of the flowers is more intricately detailed. Beneath the cushions the seats are caned, although upholstered examples also exist.

83

CHAISES-LONGUES

*Regency faux rosewood chaise-longue with gilded decoration
c.1815; max ht 34in/84cm, lgth 83in/211cm; value range C-E.*

Identification checklist for Regency chaises-longues
1. Is the chaise longue rosewood or *faux* rosewood (painted to simulate rosewood)?
2. Is the form elegant and stylish?
3. Is the frame original?
4. Does it have sabre legs?
5. Are the casters stylistically right for the period (see p. 113)?

Chaises-longues
The chaise-longue, a fully upholstered chair with an elongated seat and inclined back open at one end, was first seen during the Regency and became popular throughout Europe and the United States. Many Regency examples had painted, carved, or stencilled decoration. During the early Regency designs, although ornate, are relatively light and elegant with flowing lines incorporating scrolls, and with sabre legs (all features of the piece shown *above*). By the George IV period they had become much heavier, with a renewed emphasis on carving. Designs of this period bordered at times on the bizarre, reflecting the Prince Regent's taste for the exotic: dolphins, sphinxes, crocodiles and chinamen are among the motifs that appear

during this "high Regency" period. Prices vary dramatically: the buying criterion is elegance, as chaises-longues are essentially decorative pieces. Original decoration is an added bonus. Size is also a factor – many chaises-longues are just too large for the average house.

Reupholstery
The example above has been well reupholstered. The condition of the upholstery is important as it is very expensive to replace. Reupholstery should be carried out using taut webbing rather than springing, although in the late 19th and 20thC many chaises-longues (and settees) were reupholstered using springs, which can give an overstuffed look, whereas webbed upholstery is tighter. The framework should be original (see pp. 82-3).

Painted decoration

Painted pieces were particularly popular during the Regency. They rarely incorporate carving and the decorative details are either painted on or applied in the form of gilt metal mounts, or a combination of gilt and painting. The chaise *above* has been painted to resemble rosewood, the most commonly simulated wood. An alternative piece might have been in rosewood with ormolu mounts, but here the ormolu decoration is simulated as well. The motifs on the front rail are typically Regency – honeysuckle and anthemion are commonly found in decoration at this time.

* Furniture with paintwork has often had to be extensively redecorated. Some pieces, such as this chaise-longue, retain most of their original paintwork, but a degree of redecoration is inevitable: the amount that is acceptable is a matter of personal preference. However, even total redecoration is often considered quite acceptable – for example, where the original decoration had deteriorated beyond redemption, or the piece has been inappropriately redecorated during Victorian times or later.

Condition

The chaise-longue was made in several sections which have shrunk, causing the wood to open slightly at the joints. This is relatively minor and should not detract from the value.

American chaise-longue, c.1825-30, with typically heavy form

A boat-shaped English chaise-longue of the Regency period

VICTORIAN CHAIRS

A fine mid-19thC English rosewood library chair
c.1850; ht 39in/99cm; value range D-F

Identification checklist for mid-19thC chairs
1. Is the chair walnut, rosewood or mahogany?
2. Is it of bold and shapely design?
3. Does it have upholstery with deep buttoning?
4. Does it have cabriole legs?
5. Is it ornately carved?
6. Is the timber of high quality?
7. Does the design show a French influence (see *right*)?

Victorian chairs

Victorian (and William IV) period chairs are often very well made although they may lack the style and elegance of earlier chairs. Prices are still relatively low and are bound to rise sharply over the next few years. The balloon-back type was the most common (see pp. 80-1); the scoop-back library chair *above* (sometimes known in England as a grandfather chair) is another popular type. It would originally have formed part of a suite comprising a sofa, an armchair, and chairs without arms. Footstools were occasionally included as well. Suites are rare

today; even pairs of armchairs are uncommon, and command a premium. Scoop-back chairs were very popular in the United States, where they were made with open arms or upholstered sides, and with very elaborate carving and profile. The chair *above* exemplifies the move during the first half of the 19thC toward increasingly heavier and more exuberant furniture designs, and the return of the cabriole leg with a French scroll foot. As well as rosewood, these chairs were also made in walnut and mahogany. Reproductions exist but are obviously modern.

The French style

During the mid-19thC much
English and American furniture
was influenced by French
designs, especially those from the
Louis XV period. In England it
was a style that was adopted by
the top London cabinet-makers,
so quality tends to be high.
Typical French-style features of
the chair on the previous page
include:
* cabriole legs that flow from the
carved and shaped seat rail
* shaped uprights
* scrolled and padded arms
* the general style of carving.

The carving

The bold and ornate carving is
typical of the Victorian period and
would never be mistaken for
earlier work. The quality of the
carving will be a major factor in
the value: here it is very high, but
do not expect all examples to be
to this standard.

Condition

Below the joint there is evidence
of a small split in the top rail.
However, it is fairly slight and will
not be detrimental to value.

Upholstery

The seat, at one time sprung, is
now upholstered over taut
webbing, as it would originally
have been.

William IV chairs

The Victorian chair developed out
of the more restrained style of
William IV furniture, exemplified
by this mahogany library armchair
from c.1835, with a scoop-back,
carved arms and carved turned
legs terminating in original brass
casters. This was a period of
transition between the lighter
styles of the 18thC and the
ornateness of the Victorians.

Captain's chairs

This type of William IV/early
Victorian walnut armchair is
popularly known in England as a
captain's chair. The leather
upholstery, turned spindles in the
back and the bold ring-turned
legs are typical. Oak examples are
slightly less desirable than those
in walnut. Examples by top
makers may have a stamp
underneath one of the seat rails.
The leather upholstery, although
unlikely to be original, should
ideally be old, and in good
condition, as it is expensive to
replace.

TABLES

The earliest "tables" were simply boards placed on trestles, but during the 15thC the improvement of joinery techniques made possible the development of "table boards" with permanent sub-frames.

The first table to be made by a joiner was a standing low cupboard on extended legs, or stiles, and was used for serving food and for storage. Gradually, the space below the table top was reduced to a shallow frieze which enabled the table to be sat at in relative comfort. The legs were united by stretchers.

Until the beginning of the 18thC most tables, apart from those specifically intended for dining (see pp. 114-131), were small, multi-purpose side tables. These were in oak until the mid-17thC and also in walnut from c.1660; some had a folding top. Before 1660 designs were straightforward and solid, with Gothic carving. After the Restoration styles became more adventurous and ornate, reflecting French and Dutch tastes, and with a greater emphasis on the decorative aspect. Barley twists for legs and shaped stretchers were popular, and there was a host of new turnings (see pp. 110-11). During the 17thC American styles followed the English, although maple and pine were used in addition to walnut and oak.

Tables from the second half of the 17thC are still quite readily available although, as with all categories of furniture, good pieces are becoming increasingly scarce and as a result are highly priced. However, many are still surprisingly inexpensive and represent good value – for example, small oak side tables with simple turnings and moulded stretchers.

The earliest table specifically designed for card- and game-playing was introduced toward the end of the 17thC. These are commonly circular, with a folding top; the legs are united by flat shaped stretchers and two of the back legs pivot out to support the top. By the turn of the century the cabriole leg was in fashion and stretchers were dropped. Card and games tables now generally had rectangular tops, with protruding roundels at the corners for candlesticks, and wells for money or counters.

Other tables with specific functions, such as writing tables, were also introduced during this period. The lowboy or dressing table first appeared during the early years of the 18thC, sometimes with a walnut or japanned toilet mirror to sit on top. Many Queen Anne-period lowboys are quite simple in outline, relying for decorative effect on highly figured, mellow walnut veneers, restrained carving and flowing cabriole legs; these are among the most classic pieces of English furniture. Good examples of fine colour and patina are becoming increasingly hard to find.

The Queen Anne style became established in the United States in c.1730. The lowboy was particularly popular and remained a high-fashion piece well into the American

Chippendale period; many incorporate a carved shell motif.

Several new forms were introduced during the Chippendale period, among them the China table, the pembroke table and night or bedside tables, which are particularly popular in pairs, although these are rare. There was also a growing demand for the tea or tripod table as the fashion for tea-drinking spread. Until ten years ago tripod tables were very common and only those with a dished top, a pie-crust edge and carving to the base could be expected to be highly priced. Today, the tripod table with a plain top is also collectable provided that the proportions, colour and condition are good.

Mahogany tables of this period are found either in the solid or partially veneered. The best are crisply carved, with a good colour and patina.

Another popular Chippendale form is the urn table, or kettle stand, made until c.1800. These are very sought-after today as occasional tables; many have a pull-out slide on which to stand a saucer or teabowl.

Centre and drum tables were popular from c.1760 until the mid-19thC and are used mainly as decorative pieces to stand in halls or drawing rooms, although drum tables were initially designed for writing at in the library.

Pembroke and sofa tables are associated with the late 18thC (although the pembroke was introduced during the Chippendale period), when lighter styles were in vogue. The sofa table, a longer, narrower version of the pembroke, was designed to stand in front of a sofa and was used originally for ladies to write, draw or read at. Most are in mahogany. Exotic woods such as satinwood were also frequently used, principally in veneered form. Marquetry decoration of Neo-classical design is found on the finer pieces, with crossbanding and inlay replacing the carving found on earlier tables.

Work tables, specifically designed for embroidery and needlework, were introduced during the second half of the 18thC. These contain compartments for sewing accoutrements and are usually fitted with a silk bag. Most silk bags found today are replacements. "Nests" of tables, usually comprising three or four tables of graduated size, became fashionable at this time, and were popular again in the Edwardian period.

Console and pier tables were made throughout Europe during the 18th and 19thC. Many had marble tops and ornate gilt bases. Elegant occasional tables were also made in France, Scandinavia and Holland; the French examples sometimes incorporate porcelain plaques. As with other types of furniture, American tables of the early 19thC show the influence of the French Empire style.

Victorian tables, mostly in walnut, are characteristically robust and often supported on ornately carved pedestal or platform bases. Some have French-style ormolu mounts and other embellishments.

EARLY CARD AND GAMES TABLES

An English George II Virginia walnut games table
c.1730; ht 29in/73.5cm; wdth 36in/91.5cm; value range C-E.

Identification checklist for 18thC card and games tables
1. Is the table Virginia walnut or mahogany?
2. Are the top and legs made in the solid with a veneered frieze?
3. Does the table have carved decoration?
4. Does it have circular corners dished for candlesticks, and wells for counters?
5. Does it have a concertina-action base or a gateleg support?
6. Are the legs well-shaped cabrioles?
7. Does the table have claw-and-ball feet?

Card tables
The earliest type of card or games table was introduced at the end of the 17thC, and was usually oak or walnut-veneered, with a half-round folding top and turned tapering legs united by flat stretchers. One or both of the back legs swung out to support the top. In the early 18thC the cabriole leg was introduced, and from this date the design remained basically the same. Pedestal versions were made during the Regency and Victorian periods. A popular 18thC American type had a serpentine top and five legs, one of which swung round to support the top.

Ear pieces
Ear pieces, the shaped pieces at the tops of the cabrioles, are often not original. They are invariably made separately from the rest of the leg to prevent excessive wastage of timber and are then simply glued on. They are thus prone to being knocked off and lost. Although there is always a seam where the ear piece joins the leg – even with original ear pieces – it is nearly always possible to detect a replacement by comparing the colour of the timber, the patination, and any carving with the rest of the table. Ideally, at least some of the ear pieces should be original.

The top

The shape of the top, which is made in the solid, is typical of the period. The rounded projecting corners (sometimes known as castellated ends) indicate that internally there are candle stands – a quality feature.

* Examine the underside of the flap (or lower flap if there are more than one): there should be shadowing in those areas where it overhangs the base and has been exposed to the air and the natural oils of the hand.
* The arc made by the gateleg as it travels across the underside should also be visible (see p. 123).

Screws

Steel screws were used in the 18thC and are a good aid to dating. They are hand-made and the thread runs right up to the head, unlike modern screws which are machine-made and have a part-thread, part-plain shank.

Claw-and-ball feet

Claw-and-ball feet were very popular in the first half of the 18thC; this foot, from the table in the main picture, is one of the best types, as the claw appears to grip the ball tightly. In reproductions the claw often appears to sit limply on the ball.

* Expect signs of knocks or damage around the feet, especially on any carving. The undersides will be pitted.

Versatility

The table has two flaps, providing a choice of surface. The top flap opens to reveal a green baize surface suitable for card-playing; beneath this is the flap with the chess board, visible in the main picture. The deep frieze contains a useful storage area for cards, counters, chess pieces, and so on.

* Most card and games tables have a single baize top; the type shown here, with a choice of surfaces, is more desirable. The most sought-after, and rarest, type is that with a triple-top.

Cabriole legs

The carving is crisp, with a natural build-up of dirt and wax in the crevices. The quality of the carving is indicative of the piece as a whole. The cabriole leg was used on Victorian reproductions, but the shape is often exaggerated and the carving may lack the crispness of the original.

The concertina action

Card and games tables of the 17th and 18thC are usually supported on one or two gatelegs. When the table is opened these are not equally spread. A more desirable alternative, generally associated with carved tables of the early-mid-18thC, such as the one shown on these pages, is the concertina action, whereby the two back legs, united by a stretcher, pull away from each other toward the ends of the table so that all four legs are positioned at the corners when the table is open. This results in a more aesthetically pleasing appearance than the gateleg type of table.

LOWBOYS

An early 18thC English walnut lowboy
c.1715; ht 27³/4 in/70.5cm; wdth 29in/73.5cm; value range B-D

Identification checklist for early 18thC lowboys
1. Is the table walnut?
2. Does it have cabriole legs with pad feet?
3. Is it veneered (apart from the legs, which should be in the solid)?
4. Does it have a quarter-veneered top?
5. Does it have cross banding and feather banding (see p. 14)?
6. Does it have ovolo moulding and/or re-entrant corners?
7. Are the drawer linings relatively narrow compared with pieces from the 17thC, and in oak or pine?
8. Are the handles original?

Lowboys
Originally used as dressing tables, these pieces are among the most classic types of early 18thC English furniture. The most sought-after examples are those that are veneered. They were also made in the solid in oak and other country woods, and, during the Chippendale period, in Virginia walnut and mahogany. Some lowboys are found with straight legs: examples from the Chippendale period in mahogany with carved spandrels are often of very fine quality. Those of a similar quality but with cabriole legs tend to fetch higher prices.
92

Handles
The handles of the lowboy are stylistically right for the period but close examination reveals the faint outline of another handle, proving that the current ones are not original to the piece.

Quarter veneering

Typically for the period, the top is quarter-veneered in burr walnut, that is, the veneers are laid in four mirrored or bookmatched sections.

* Burrs, especially the tighter ones, are generally more sought-after than figured veneers, which in turn are more desirable than straight-grained veneers.
* Tops have occasionally been reveneered or replaced altogether. Make sure that the same wood has been used throughout and that any decorative details on the drawer fronts correspond with any on the top in terms of dimension, style and colour.
* The outside edge is cross-banded, with an ovolo (quarter-round) moulding, and re-entrant corners – desirable features found in the first half of the 18thC.
* The pleasant honey colour and good old surface and patina greatly enhance the value of this piece.

Woodworm

The legs, which are well-shaped cabrioles, show some signs of worm. However, it is a minor infestation which is not active and should therefore not be regarded as a problem.

* If worm is active, fresh pale powder will be evident in the bore holes.
* There is a small crack in the veneer just above the leg; this is fairly common for a piece of this age.

The carcass

Remove one or all of the drawers and examine the carcass from the inside where it has not been veneered: typically, pine has been used as the base wood of this lowboy. A small natural split is also visible in the side panel, a blemish which should show itself, however faintly, on the outer surface.

* If a severe old split is visible on the interior and there is no sign of it from the outside, the piece has almost certainly been reveneered at a later date (see p. 16).

Construction

This detail from the lowboy shows how the legs are secured to the top sections: the sides and front of the piece are tenoned into the top of the legs and strengthened by pine glue blocks. The underside looks reassuringly old and undisturbed.

Feet

The lower part of the foot shows the expected signs of age and is darker than the upper part – the result of a natural build-up of dirt; a few knocks and scratches are visible.

SIDE TABLES

*A late 17thC English oak side table
c.1670; ht 28¹/₂in/72cm; wdth 32in/81cm; value range D-F*

Identification checklist for 17thC side tables
1. Is the table oak?
2. Is it of joined construction, using pegs and tenons (see p. 12)?
3. Are any pegs hand-made, that is, irregular in shape and standing slightly proud of the surface?
4. Is the top original?
5. Is any carving irregular and obviously done by hand?
6. Are the drawer linings chunky?
7. Does the grain on the drawer bottom run from front to back?
8. Is the back unfinished?

Side tables
Side tables have been made virtually throughout the history of furniture-making and exist in many different styles and woods. Early examples, from the 16th and 17thC, always have stretchers; it is not until the Queen Anne period that side tables were made without them. The Charles II oak side table *above* is of high quality and has a good rich colour. The basic outline is typical of the period but a side table of lesser quality will probably be without carving to the drawer, and the stretcher formation will be less complex, relying on plain or simply moulded stretchers to unite the legs.

Quality features
Features that lift this table above the ordinary and enhance its value include:
* carved drawer front
* ball-and-reel turned frame (rather than plain stretchers)
* "H-confirmation" stretcher at the base, with high stretchers front and back
* warm rich colour, with good old surface
* pleasing proportions
* nicely executed ball feet in reasonable condition.

The top
Typically, the top, *above*, is made up of two boards; a slight split has been caused by one of the pegs that secured it to the structure below. The fixing pegs on the table top should be in line with this structure.
* The moulding around the table top is a typical 17thC feature.
* Examine the top from the underside as you would the pegged top of a joined stool (see pp. 50-51): it should look unpolished and dry. The outer edges that overhang the frame will be darker in appearance – the result of being handled over the years. There should be no signs or holes to suggest that the top has been on another table.

Construction
Glue blocks, *above*, are visible from the back when the drawer is removed: these were used in addition to the pegs to join the top to the sides. A drawer stop is also visible, and a metal bracket – this is a somewhat crude attempt to keep the joined boards of the top level.
* Side tables are left relatively unfinished at the back, as they were intended to stand against the walls of a room and thus the back would not be visible.

Drawers
The drawers of 17thC side tables are constructed in the same way as those of chests of the period (see p. 25), either held together with bold dovetails or simply nailed using hand-made nails (which have large heads and are irregular in shape). The grain of the drawer base runs from front to back. The sides of the drawers will be approximately 3/4in (2cm) thick and will have chanelled side runners. Side table drawers are usually without locks.

Feet
The ball feet of early tables are often heavily rotted and the undersides may appear very pitted – the result of standing on damp old floors. In severe cases the rotten areas may have been cut away (thereby reducing the height of the piece). In some instances the whole foot below the stretcher block will have been replaced. This is not as serious as a replaced or partially replaced top, drawer or leg, but should be allowed for in the price.

Mid-18thC side table
This is a good example of a mid-18thC Chippendale-period mahogany side table, c.1755, with a number of features characteristic of the period:
* the frieze and the square legs, both decorated with blind fret carving of chinoiserie design
* the shape of the legs, which terminate in block feet
* the use of mahogany (on fashionable furniture)
* the lack of stretchers
* the very English appearance.
The table shows well the lighter and darker areas associated with antique furniture, with the more prominent surfaces being paler. The front feet display evidence of knocks and scuffs. This is a fine example; tables of similar form but without the carved decoration will be more common and consequently, less expensive.

TRIPOD TABLES

An English Chippendale-period mahogany tripod table
c.1755; ht 27³/₄in/70.5cm; dia 29¹/₄in/74cm; value range E–F

Identification checklist for 18thC tripod tables
1. Is the table mahogany?
2. Is it made in the solid?
3. Do the top and bottom belong together (see opposite)?
4. Is there any carved decoration?
5. Does the table rest on a baluster column?
(Alternatives are reeded, leaf-carved or gun-barrel.)
6. Are the legs and top well-proportioned, with a good
spread to the base?
7. Does the table top either tilt or rotate?

Variations
* Country-made tripod tables are
found in oak, fruitwoods and elm.
* Although the tops of the best
tripod tables are made from one
piece of timber, in many perfectly
good examples they are made up
96

of three joined boards.

American tripod tables
Tripod tables were popular with
American cabinet-makers. They
were often made in mahogany
and cherry.

Tripod tables

The tripod table was introduced in England during the 1730s, and was most popular in the Chippendale period. Most are found in the solid, although some small occasional tripod tables of the late 18thC are veneered. Tops are usually round, although square and oval examples also exist.

Feet

The sole underneath the foot is an invariable sign of quality. The casters are original and even retain the original leather around the wheel (a feature which is sometimes found on small casters of the 18thC).

The tilt-top mechanism

Except in the smallest tripods, the tops are made so that they can tilt to a vertical position allowing the table to be stored in a corner of the room when not in use. Typically, the base of the table shown on the previous page tenons into a block at the top of the column. The top is fixed by means of two bearers and held in place with a brass catch. There should be signs on the underside of the top where it has rested on the block.

Bird-cage mechanism

Many tilt-top tables of the period have a "bird-cage" support, as in the example *above*. The bird-cage is fixed to the underside of the table top and the whole mechanism slots into the top of the pedestal. A peg through the stem allows the top to rotate, tilt, or be fixed in place. (The marks around the edge of the top were made by a sewing instrument that was once attached to the table.)

Dished tops

Many tripod table tops have been dished, or hollowed out, from a plain top at a later date to increase the value of the table. As tripod table tops are relatively shallow, the screws that attach the bearers to the top sit just below the surface. If a top has been dished out, its thickness will be reduced and the screw-holes will show through. However skilfully these holes are plugged, they cannot be disguised against close inspection.

Construction

The cabriole legs of tripod tables are made individually and dovetailed into the central column, *above*. They may be strengthened from underneath with a wrought-iron bracket.

PEMBROKE TABLES

A late 18thC English mahogany pembroke table
c.1785; ht 28in/71cm, lgth 37in/94cm; value range B-F

Identification checklist for late 18thC pembroke tables
1. Is the table veneered, possibly in rosewood or satinwood, rather than in the solid?
2. Does it have marquetry decoration?
3. Does the table have cross-banding or inlays?
4. Are decorative motifs in keeping with the period?
5. Are the legs slender and tapered?
6. Is the table oval (or serpentine) in shape?
7. Are any drawers mahogany-lined?
8. Is there a dummy drawer at the back?

Pembroke tables
Pembroke tables (precursors of sofa tables – see pp. 100-1) were first seen in England during the Chippendale period, when they were usually mahogany, with carved decoration; tops were either rectangular or of "butterfly" (serpentine) outline. By the last quarter of the 18thC the oval shape had become very fashionable, and styles were lighter; veneered examples replaced those in the solid, and decoration was inlaid or sometimes painted, rather than carved. Bow-fronted tops were popular during this period. From the early 19thC pembroke tables became less fashionable and consequently, were not as finely made as those of the 18thC.

Signs of quality
The quality and therefore the price of pembroke tables varies enormously. The exceptionally fine example *above* will command a premium. Its desirable features include:
* elegant square tapering legs
* inlaid flutes to the top of the legs
* the drawer, which is lined in mahogany and reflects the bow shape of the top
* attractive cross-banded decoration, which runs along the edge of the central section and between the flaps
* the extensive marquetry decoration and the characteristic oval fan with scorched shading
* the inlaid dummy drawer on the back of the table.

Condition

The hinged wooden bearers that support the flaps are beech, which is prone to worm; replacements are not uncommon, and are acceptable provided that the work has been well done. The flaps are prone to warping and splitting: butterfly joints have been inset on the underside of this table to hold the split boards in place – such legitimate restoration need not cause undue concern.

* The flaps of some larger pembroke tables are supported by two bearers rather than one.

* The legs of pembroke tables tend to be particularly fragile – look for signs of breaks and splits.

Authenticity

A reassuring sign of age and authenticity is the mark visible around the edge of the flap, *above*, caused by the swing of the bearer.

Reproductions

Pembroke tables were often reproduced in England in the Sheraton style during the late Victorian and Edwardian periods. Reproductions can be identified by the use of machine-cut rather than hand-cut veneers (see p. 10); the sentimental nature of any painted decoration; and the screws, which are made by machine rather than by hand (see p. 12). However, a few examples from this period are of extremely high quality. These are highly sought-after today and command ever-rising prices.

Inlay

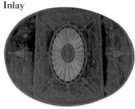

Marquetry inlays are sometimes restored or replaced. If the inlay becomes wet, damage can occur as the glue dries out, causing the sections to loosen. The glue may also become over-dry through excessive exposure to sun or central heating. The central section of this table top has been completely replaced. The detail, *above bottom*, shows the panel without its original inlay but ready for restoration. Recent inlay is relaid within a press and is very flat, with tight joints. Old marquetry has a raised surface where shrinkage and movement have occurred over the years. The new panel, *above top*, has no such ripples. It can also be identified as recent because, although competently restored, the colours are not as rich as the original ones that survive outside the panel.

* The Neo-classical inlay with its urns, swags and other characteristic motifs, is typical of the late 18thC. The inlay contains a variety of woods, including boxwood, harewood, satinwood and green-dyed sycamore. The central fan is also very typical of the period.

American pembroke tables

Pembroke tables were popular in the United States. Many date from the American Chippendale period. The most usual type has a rectangular or serpentine-shaped top and square chamfered legs with shaped flat cross-stretchers, frequently enhanced by pierced decoration.

SOFA TABLES

An early 19thC English rosewood sofa table
c.1810; ht 28³/₄in/73cm; lgth 58in/147cm; dpth 24in/61cm; value range B-E

Identification checklist for 19thC end-support sofa tables
1. Is the table in rosewood or another good quality wood?
2. Is it veneered?
3. Does it have a combination of real and dummy drawers?
4. Does the table have a turned stretcher?
5. Are the end-supports original? (See "Improvements".)
6. Does the table have applied gilt brass mounts?
7. Does it have ornate casters?

Sofa tables
The sofa table, originally designed to stand behind a sofa, evolved from the pembroke table (see pp. 98-9) in the last quarter of the 18thC, but is narrower and longer. Sofa tables usually have drawers at the front with dummy drawers behind (being too shallow for real drawers on both sides). Late 18thC examples are principally in mahogany or, to a lesser degree, satinwood or more exotic woods. The best examples are veneered, with crossbanding and inlaid stringing. Some Regency examples have fine metal mounts. Sofa tables continued to be made, in smaller numbers, until the mid-19thC, although quality declined

somewhat. Victorian and Edwardian examples tend to copy earlier styles. Sofa tables from the Sheraton period are the most sought-after.

Stretchers
Stretchers on early 19thC sofa tables are usually turned, like that shown *above*. A high stretcher is generally preferred to those positioned at the base of the supports. Late 18thC stretchers are plain.

Note
While width is fairly constant, the depth varies somewhat from about 22-30in (56-76cm). The narrower variety usually commands higher prices.

Condition
Shrinkage is sometimes a problem on sofa tables: if the top shrinks it can cause the flap to stand out slightly when unsupported, as it does here, rather than hang down straight. The weight of the flap can also put pressure on the top, causing it to split.

Supports
A variety of different supports were used on sofa tables. In the late 18thC supports were relatively plain. Lyre-end-supports were used during the Regency period. From c.1815 end-supports on a platform base with a carved foot became popular (see *below*).

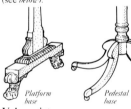

Platform base   *Pedestal base*

Value point
Sofa tables with end supports are more sought-after than the later type of pedestal sofa table, which can be quite heavy and inelegant.

"Improvements"
The less elegant versions from the 1820s and 30s are sometimes "improved" by making new legs, converted from the end supports of cheval mirrors, to resemble those of the more fashionable Regency period tables. Check that the colour of any end-supports matches that of the rest of the piece. Look for signs of interference on the underside of the table. Marks in the centre may have been made by a central pedestal, now removed.

Feet
The applied gilt metal mounts are typical of early 19thC sofa tables, and are in keeping with the ornate styles of the period.

Handles
When the handle of the table is unscrewed the wood beneath it appears undisturbed – a sign that it is original.
* Rosewood, in which this table is veneered, was at its most popular in the early 19thC. The original colour is visible when the handle is removed, but elsewhere the table has developed a good, slightly faded colour. Rosewood can vary enormously; at its worst it may be very black, especially if it has been inexpertly repolished – rosewood is one of the most difficult woods to repolish successfully.
* The escutcheon is rounded at the bottom, indicating a date earlier than c.1870.

Repairs
Damaged table tops are sometimes replaced. Observe the direction of the grain: on an original top the grain runs across the depth of the table rather than along its width.

WORK TABLES

An English Regency-period work table
c.1810/15; ht 29¹⁄₂in/75cm, full lgth 32³⁄₄in/83cm; value range D-E.

Identification checklist for Regency work tables
1. Is the table veneered in a high-quality wood?
2. Is it more ornate than the restrained simplicity of late 18thC furniture?
3. Does it have a platform base?
4. Does it have scroll feet? (Lesser pieces might have simple turned bun feet.)
5 Are the drawer linings slender and in mahogany, with fine dovetails?
6. Does the table have applied gilt metal mounts?
7. Is it freestanding and therefore with a polished back?

Signs of quality
The table *above* has two particularly fine features:
* coromandel veneers
* gilt metal mounts.

Work tables
These were introduced in the late 18thC, primarily for ladies to sew at. Usually fairly small and compact, they are fitted with a silk bag and compartments for needles, cotton, and so on. Some have lift-up tops with fitted interiors. Most of those from the late 18thC stand on four square tapering or slender turned legs. Pedestal supports and turned fluted legs are typical of the early 19thC, as is the desirable type with lyre-shaped supports. As the 19thC progressed work tables began to be produced in larger quantities and in a greater range of quality, many being cheaply made and devoid of embellishments or carving. Victorian work tables are characterized by their use of walnut; the best are veneered with tight burr veneers and incorporate intricate inlaid decoration. The pull-out "bags" in this period are usually of solid form, and veneered. Another Victorian type is that of conical form terminating in a carved tripod support and in walnut or papier mâché with mother-of-pearl and gilt embellishments.

Handles and drawers

Although there are no marks
around the handles to indicate
that they are not original, they are
in fact modern reproductions: the
original axe-head drop handles
would have been more finely
made, with a finer shank.
Although stylistically correct, the
knobs are always modern
replacements.
* The handles of any dummy
drawers on back of the table
should always be checked, even if
the handles on the working
drawers have been established as
original.

Construction

The table was, typically, made in
separate sections: the top screws
into the column and the column is
tenoned into the base, with the
joints visible on the underside.

Flaps

The underside of the flap has
been stained dark so that it is less
conspicuous when it hangs down.
The marks made by the bracket
as it is opened and closed are
visible on the underside, and are a
good sign of authenticity.
* The flaps of the table are
hinged with a rule joint, which is
neater when the flaps are down
than the standard joint, and is a
sign of quality.

Late 18thC work table

This late 18thC work table is
characterized by its very French-
influenced form, especially in the
shape of the legs, and typifies the
elegant and restrained style of the
late 18thC. Work tables on four
legs from this period are often
accompanied by an under-tier as
this one is. It is also fitted with a
drawer that pulls out from the
side rather than from the front.
These drawers are usually fitted
out with various compartments.
Typically for its period, the table
is made in mahogany, partially in
the solid and partially veneered.
An additional feature is the pull-
up slide, infilled with pleated silk,
designed to protect the user from
the glare of the fire – a feature
associated with work tables of the
late 18thC.
* Tables in this style also exist in
satinwood and other exotic woods,
such as kingwood.
* Alternative forms of support
include slender, square tapering
legs, perhaps with a spade foot,
and slender turned legs,
sometimes with reeded
decoration. Legs usually
terminate in casters.

Condition

The main pitfalls with work
tables is the degree of restoration
they may have undergone. The
legs are particularly vulnerable
and may show evidence of breaks
or repairs. Sometimes a whole leg
has had to be replaced: examine
and compare each one carefully
for inconsistencies in the colour
and grain of wood, and for signs of
breaks. Slides are sometimes
removed. Handles are often
replaced (see p. 13). Sliding pull-
out work bags and pull-up slides
are frequently relined: original
silk is rare.

DRUM TABLES

An English Regency-period mahogany drum table
c.1810-15; ht 29³/₄in/75.5cm; dia 48in/122cm; value range B-D

Identification checklist for Regency drum tables
1. Is the table veneered in rosewood or mahogany?
2. Does it have a turned central pedestal base?
3. Do the pedestal and the table top belong together (see facing page)?
4. Is the carcass either oak or pine?
5. Do real drawers alternate with dummy drawers?
6. Does the table have a leathered or veneered top?

Note
Although most drum tables are veneered in mahogany or rosewood, exceptionally fine examples are sometimes found in more exotic woods such as satinwood and kingwood, and these usually command higher prices.

Drum tables
These freestanding tables, also known as library or writing tables, were introduced around the mid-18thC and are characterized by their deep frieze, which contains the drawers. Today they are sometimes used as centre tables in halls, or lobbies, although true centre tables have no drawers.

Drum tables often have revolving tops and some of the earlier examples have lettered drawers to facilitate filing. Size varies; the example *above* is fairly standard.
* A variant of the drum table, known as a rent table, is supported on a square cabinet with access gained from above.

Tops
Tops are usually leathered; most of those found today are replacements. Drum tables with a veneered top are generally less sought-after.

Construction
The pedestal base is made separately from the top, which simply sits on the base: a "peg" on top of the column, *above,* slots into a hole in the block fixed to the underside of the table top (see *below*), holding it securely in place but enabling rotation. This four-splay solid pedestal with knees provides a good indication of the date of the piece as it is of a style not introduced until c.1810. It is of high quality, banded to match the drawers and top. The plain squared toe-caps (see main picture) are also desirable. (Lion's-paw feet would be an alternative.)

Supports
Most drum tables are supported on a central pedestal base, the style of which is the most reliable indication of the date of the piece: the classic 18thC pedestal has a gun-barrel stem with a plain elegant sweep; in the first half of the 19thC the supports were heavy with more turning, exemplified by the table shown here. Later 19thC examples have a central pedestal support on a platform base.

gun-barrel stem   *platform base*

Authenticity
Pedestals and tops are sometimes mismatched: check that the block on the underside of the table top is undisturbed-looking, as this example is (*above*), with no sign of another block having been there, and with no spare or plugged holes.
* A useful sign of authenticity is repeated decoration, in this case on the table top and on the pedestal base (see main picture).

Drawers
Real drawers usually alternate with dummy or false drawers. Alternatively, instead of dummy drawers there may be four or more wedge-shaped drawers. These can be impractical and awkward to use and, because they are narrow at the back, tend to fall out as they are being opened.

COMMODES

*A late 18thC English mahogany commode, or bedside table
c.1785; max ht 32in/81cm; width 22in/56cm; value range E.-F*

Identification checklist for 18thC commodes
1. Is the commode mahogany?
2. Is the front applied with astragal moulding?
3. Does the commode have a tray top or an overhanging flat top?
4. Does the gallery have pierced decoration?
5. Is the commode made in one piece?
6. Are the legs square?
7. Is the back neatly finished?

Commodes
The commode, or night table (as it was known in the 18thC), was introduced c.1750 and continued to be made during a large part of the later 18thC, becoming lighter in style as the century progressed. The example shown *above* is of fairly average size for this type of furniture. Commodes are no longer put to their original use, but are popular mostly as bedside tables, or as stands for phones, televisions and so on. Some commodes are shaped below the cupboard.

Commodes are not known to have been much faked. They are still relatively modestly priced but
106

have become much more expensive in the last five years. In pairs (which are scarce) they are among the most saleable pieces of furniture today, especially those in satinwood with inlay and/or a tambour-fronted door.

Signs of quality
This commode has several fine features:
* the matching flamed veneers on the doors
* the pierced decoration of the galleried tray top
* carrying handles cut out from the top
* a shallow top drawer, a nice additional feature.

Interior
The commode drawer, which pulls out from beneath the cupboard, retains its original fittings. Such fittings are sometimes removed and replaced by a leathered top. This does not affect the value.

Construction
The commode is, typically, constructed in one piece. The front legs "split" when the commode drawer is opened. All four legs are invariably square. The cupboard fronts are applied with the astragal moulding typical of the period.

Authenticity
A good sign of authenticity is the mark on the inside of the carcass revealed when the top drawer is removed; this corresponds to the width of the drawer rail and has obviously built up over a long period.

Other types of commode furniture:
* The commode chair, popular during the Chippendale period and based on an elbow chair; the pot was hidden by a deep shaped frieze to the front and side rails of the chair (see p. 67).
* The commode chest, which resembles a small chest, but has four dummy drawers. The hinged top and two of the top dummy drawers lift up for use. Many of these items have been converted into small chests, with the dummy drawers replaced by real drawers with new linings. Such reworking should be readily apparent on inspection.
* Commode steps. These take the form of bed steps and today make very good bedside tables.
* Pot cupboards (*below*), intended simply to hold a pot. They are very sought-after today as they make ideal small bedside tables. Price will depend on quality, which ranges from very fine sophisticated pieces, perhaps in satinwood with inlay and/or a tabmour fronted door, to very simple examples, which can still be obtained for modest sums.

Later styles
By the end of the 18thC styles were more restrained. This pot cupboard is typical in its use of satinwood, its gently tapering legs, galleried top and tambour front, which comprises strips of satinwood and purpleheart.
* Purpleheart is a rare wood commonly associated with high-quality furniture of the late 18thC. When fresh and unpolished it is quite purple in colour, but in time turns to brown.
* Overhanging flat tops were sometimes used instead of the tray top.

VICTORIAN CARD TABLES

*An English Victorian-period card table
c.1860; ht 29in/73.5cm; wdth 38in/98cm; value range E-F*

Identification checklist for Victorian card tables
1. Is the table walnut?
2. Is it carved, perhaps quite elaborately?
3. Is the top highly figured?
4. Does the table have a central pedestal?
5. Is the carving darker in inaccessible areas where there is a build-up of dirt and polish?
6. Does the piece have characteristically bold overall proportions?
7. Does the top swivel?

Victorian card tables
The pedestal card or games table is peculiar to the Regency and Victorian periods. (For the other types, see pp. 90-91.) They are mostly walnut, with ornate carving and generally bold proportions. Tables in the style of that shown above are sometimes known as basket tables because of the design of their base.

Signs of quality
Several features enhance the value of the table *above*:

* the serpentine-shaped top, in quarter-veneered burr walnut
* the ornateness of the basket-shaped base, and the quality of the carving. A plainer example, with a turned support and an unshaped top would be worth about a third to a half the value of this example.

Dating point
Furniture of the Victorian period and later was made using machine-made hinges and screws (see p.12).

Carving

With its sumptuous carving the table is a good example of high-Victorian furniture. The more ornate the table, the better the Victorians considered it to be. The jewelled finial is particularly Victorian. As is to be expected, the carving is darker in inaccessible areas, which do not receive much light or polish.

The interior

The Victorians paid more attention to furniture interiors than was usual in earlier periods. This interior well for storing the cards is particularly well finished.
* Tops that swivel round and then open, as that of this table does, were introduced in the early 19thC.

Note

* A walnut card table of ornate design is almost certainly Victorian: card tables were made in veneered walnut during the Queen Anne period but these are of restrained design and usually have cabriole legs. After c.1740 walnut was rarely used by English cabinet-makers until Victorian times, when styles were exuberant.
* The top and frieze are veneered with highly figured walnut. The Victorians often embellished veneering with coloured polish to highlight the figuring. However, the colour difference tends to become more pronounced over the years as the timber fades. This seldom reduces the value.

Condition

The general condition of the table is good although there is a split in the central boss (a minor defect). Despite the great weight of the table, there are no breaks in the legs. Despite the great weight of the legs, the most vulnerable part of the table: cabriole-type legs tend to break near the ankles – inspect these areas for cleverly disguised repairs.

Casters

The casters are the original ones with the ceramic wheels typical of the period. These are white but brown was often used. Casters that are counter-sunk into the feet as these are, suggest a high-quality piece.

Authenticity

Always examine the underside of the table to verify that the top belongs with the base: there should be no signs of alterations and no marks on one part that do not correspond with marks on the other.

Legs

Cup and cover 1560-1680

Doric column 1570-1700

Ringed baluster 1580-1740

Turned Tudor Gothic 16thC

Parallel baluster 1620-1740

Fluted early 17thC

Bobbin turning, 2nd half 17thC

Ball-turned 1650-1700

Barley-twist 1660-1710

Walnut part-twist mid-17thC

Walnut scroll (Continental) c.1675

Slender baluster 1660-1800

Inverted cup baluster 1675-1700

Turned inverted cup, late 17thC

Octagonal late 17thC

Double open twist late 17thC

Carved scroll, late 17thC

Double scroll, late 17thC

Scroll top (Continental) late 17thC

Portugues bulb, early 18thC

Queen Anne Cabriole legs, early 18thC

Cabriole, carved on inside of knee

Cabriole, hipped at seat level

Cabriole with shell motif

Cabriole with paw foot

Early Georgian cabriole

Cabriole mid-18thC

Cabriole with claw-and-ball foot

Cabriole with pad foot

Carved hoof foot early 18thC

Plain hoof foot c.1720

Hoof foot with pad mid-18thC

Stylized hoof foot early 18thC

Plain club foot, mid-18thC

Knurl foot mid-18thC

French cabriole late 18thC

"French" cabriole 1750-1800

Pad-foot with tapering leg, 1720-1800

Club foot with pad c.1740

Whorl foot (Continental) mid-18thC

Cloven hoof foot (Continental) mid-18thC

Straight moulded leg, mid-18thC

Chamfered 1750-80

Plain straight mid-18thC

Blind fretted mid-18thC

Cluster column mid-18thC

turned late 18thC

111

LEGS AND FEET

Adam tapered late 18thC

Slender reeded 1780-1810

Adam carved late 18thC

Adam fluted, late 18thC

Square tapered with spade foot late 18thC

Painted leg, late 18th/early 19thC

Turned and fluted c.1785

Tapered scroll 18thC

Windsor turned early 18thC

Sabre leg early 19thC

"Lion" leg, early 19thC

Victorian "Tudor" c.1845

Bracket feet, bun feet and casters

  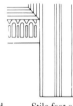

Victorian "Elizabethan" mid-19thC

Reeded mid-19thC

Stile foot of chest 17thC

Stile foot of coffer, 17th & 18thC

William and Mary bun foot, late 17thC

Flattened bun foot late 17thC

Bun foot, late 17th-early 18thC

Early bracket foot
late 17thC

Bracket foot
early 18thC

Plain bracket foot
c.1725-80

Ogee
bracket foot
mid-18thC

Splayed
bracket foot
late 18thC

Slender
turned leg
early 19thC

19thC-style
bun foot

Leather
wheel
caster
c.1750

Square
cup
caster
c.1760

Tapered
cup
caster
c.1785

Simple
brass
caster
late
18thC

Late Regency
gilt metal caster

1730-1800

2nd half 18thC

Late
18thC/early
19thC

Late
18thC/early
19thC

1780-1820

1790-1830

Lion's paw
1790-1830

DINING FURNITURE

The earliest form of dining furniture was the trestle table, used during the Middle Ages in large dining halls and refectories, where the entire household, including servants, ate together. It was very simple, consisting of two trestles supporting a boarded top, and also doubled up as a serving table. Early examples are rare today.

The refectory table evolved in the 16thC from the trestle table and was the main form of dining table until about the middle of the 17thC. Most of those on the market today date from the 17th and 18thC and are of joined construction (see pp.116-17). The basic form varied little during the period of production, the most significant differences being in the style of leg, which is therefore the best guide to dating. Genuine examples with a good colour and patina are becoming increasingly rare and expensive. Farmhouse tables also date from this period and are usually simpler, with square legs and no stretchers. The tops are made from two or three planks with cleated, or wedge-shaped, ends.

Refectory and farmhouse tables were much copied in the Victorian period. The copies often use screws that are countersunk and camouflaged by false pegs. Fakes are not uncommon.

The dresser evolved in the 17thC from the Tridarn (alternatively known as a Duodarn), basically a three-tier version of the court cupboard (see pp.22-3). The earliest examples available today date from the mid-17thC but these are few and far between, and most are from the late 17th and 18thC. Dressers were made with and without racks and both types are popular. Some have open bases with pot boards, others are enclosed – regional differences that are a study in themselves. As a general guideline, cupboard dressers are more expensive than those with open bases.

The gateleg table appeared in the mid-17thC for use in the now smaller dining room. Most are in oak; there is great excitement among collectors when a yew or walnut example appears on the market. As with refectory tables, the style of the leg is the main aid to dating, and price is very dependent on size — small gateleg tables are still moderately priced but large examples with a double gateleg action and in original condition are now beyond the reach of most buyers.

The 1730s saw the beginning of importation of mahogany from the West Indies to England and the United States. As a timber available in broad planks, its arrival brought about great changes in cabinet-making generally, and in the development of tables in particular. The gateleg type of table evolved into the type known as the drop-leaf. It was made in mahogany, using single pieces of timber for the flaps (rather than joined boards), and with cabriole legs in preference to the cumbersome stretchers. These tables are found in a range of sizes. The timber is invariably of fine quality and colour. The drop-leaf table was also particularly popular in the United States.

New forms of dining room furniture appeared in the second half of the 18thC, such as pedestal dining tables, breakfast tables, sideboards, serving tables, wine coolers and cellarets, dumb waiters for the smaller dining room, butler-trays, and smaller items such as knife boxes and plate-buckets, as well as many other useful accessories. Life had now become sophisticated, and with it, furniture-making.

The pedestal dining table was first seen around the mid-18thC and was an innovation in furniture design: for the first time a table was available that allowed all the diners to sit at it in comfort without having to avoid legs or stretchers. Mahogany was ideal for these tables, which were made with two, three, four or more pedestals, and with removable leaves. Pedestal tables remained highly popular well into the 19thC, with pedestal design becoming heavier and more ornate from c.1810. The "D"-ended extending dining table, usually in mahogany and supported on square chamfered legs, was the main alternative at this period. Today, pedestal dining tables with a good figured top, an elegant base and in original condition command a very high price. "D"-ended tables are far more affordable. Somewhat surprisingly, the pedestal dining table, unlike other English 18thC designs, especially those for chairs, did not become popular in the United States until the turn of the century.

The last quarter of the 18thC saw the introduction of the sideboard, a form traditionally accredited to Robert Adam. Sideboards are virtually always found in mahogany and, in the late 18thC, with cross banding and other decorative inlay. The sideboard provided space for cutlery and linen and often incorporated a cellaret drawer as well. It was a popular form in the United States, where the design books of London cabinet-makers and designers were available. The sideboard was made in a variety of sizes. The serpentine-fronted type was usually considered the most desirable and elegant, and is highly sought-after today. The Victorian sideboard more resembled a cabinet, as the open space beneath the central drawer was often enclosed to provide additional storage space. Although practical, these items do not have the elegance of the 18thC. Many Edwardian reproductions were made with cheaper veneers, but those by the better makers are of fine quality and are increasingly sought after.

The breakfast table was introduced in the last quarter of the 18thC. This small dining table on a single pedestal was made in large numbers during the early 19thC to furnish the small dining rooms of the ever-increasing number of town houses.

In the Victorian period walnut was favoured for the fashionable dining room, although dining tables were still generally in mahogany, with boldly fluted chunky legs. The Victorians introduced dining tables that extended by means of a cranking action and a mechanism of interlocking bearers that did away with the need for excessive numbers of legs: most have only four.

REFECTORY TABLES

A James I-period English oak refectory table
c.1620; lgth 165in/419cm; value range B-D

Identification checklist for 17thC refectory tables
1. Is the table oak?
2. Is it of joined construction?
3. Are the tenon pegs hand-made (see p. 12)?
4. Does the table have a planked top?
5. Does the top have cleated ends?
6. Does the frieze have moulded or carved decoration?
7. Does the table have cup and cover legs?
8. Are the legs united by stretchers?
9. Does the table show unmistakeable signs of wear?
10. Do the top and base belong together (see facing page)?

Refectory tables
Most refectory tables available today date from the 17th and 18thC. They are of joined construction, held together by pegged tenons. Most are of oak and stand on four legs joined by stretchers, although very long tables require two extra legs. The top is usually made from two or three planks with cleated (wedge-shaped) ends. The style of leg is the main factor in determining age (see pp. 110-13). Good refectory tables in original condition are very difficult to find. The best examples will be of good quality construction, well-figured timber, and will have developed a warm mellow colour with plenty of depth.

Fakes
Floor boards and other old timber have been used to make up new tops or replace old ones. As well as looking for the signs of authenticity listed, *right*, a "wrong" top may also be detected by circular rather than straight saw marks, indicative of timber that has been sawn since the 19thC.

Replaced tops
It is important to check that the table is not a marriage. On a genuine table whose top and base belong together:
* the quality and colour of the timber will correspond on the base and top
* the thickness of the top will be appropriate to the dimensions of the base
* both parts will show similar signs of wear and use.

However, a replaced top may be a period one that satisfies these criteria. As a further check separate the two parts and look at the underside of top: the outline of the base should be clearly visible. The outer edges will be patinated where the table has been handled, and will thus be darker than the rest of the top, which should be dry and undisturbed looking, with no plugged or spare holes (apart from any holes made when bearers were screwed to the underside to prevent the wood from opening up). There are also likely to be marks on the underside at the points where the top has sat on the legs.

116

Reproductions

Refectory tables were reproduced in the Victorian period with heavily carved legs, as copies rather than fakes intended to deceive. They were in a lesser-quality oak, which was straw-like in colour and more straight-grained than 17th and 18thC oak. The mid-19thC oak refectory table *above* is in the early 17thC style but its heavily carved supports are very much in the Victorian style. Reproductions can be identified in a number of other ways:

* they may be held together with machine-made pegs or covered screws rather than with hand-made pegs
* the signs of wear will not be so pronounced (see *right*). The base of the legs will probably be in quite good condition, as by this period tables were not left to stand on damp floors
* they usually have a single central stretcher (a desirable feature, as it makes the table easier to sit at)
* the proportions may differ – for example 17thC refectory tables are up to about 34in (86cm) wide; Victorian reproductions may be 38in (97cm) or more
* the oak may be artificially stained to make it darker.

Later refectory tables

By the second quarter of the 18thC the refectory table had ceased to be made for fashionable houses and was superseded largely by drop-leaf and pedestal dining tables. However, in provincial areas refectory or farmhouse tables, as they are commonly known, continued to be made, in oak and elm, until the second quarter of the 19thC. The example *above*, of c.1800, with square rather than turned legs, is typical. As the table is long, it retains a central stretcher, although such tables are also frequently found without stretchers. In this period they are usually plain, as this one is, rather than carved. The quality of construction is very basic; value is assessed according to colour and patina, although even the finest examples are far less expensive than those made in the 17th and 18thC.

French refectory tables

Refectory tables were made in large numbers in the French provinces throughout the 18th and 19thC, usually in chestnut and cherrywood, and have recently been imported in their thousands to Britain and the United States. They still represent very good value for money although prices are likely to rise.

Signs of wear

Genuine period tables will show unmistakeable signs of natural wear that will not be found on modern reproductions. These include:

* uneven fading
* numerous scratches and knocks on the top, which over the years will have blended in to give a natural appearance
* knocks and scratches on the stretchers, parts of which will be more worn where feet have rested on them over the years
* rotting and/or worm on the base of the legs, which may have been built up.

117

DRESSERS

An 18thC English oak dresser
c.1750; wdth 66in/167.5cm; value range B-E

Identification checklist for 18thC dressers
1. Is the table oak?
2. Is it made in the solid?
3. Is it of joined construction, using mortices and tenons, and held together with hand-made pegs?
4. Are the drawer fronts plain (unlike those of the 17thC, which have applied moulding, see p. 13)?
5. Are the baseboards made up of a number of short boards running from front to back?
6. Is there a dry and "untouched" look to the inside and back?
7. Are the dovetails relatively coarse (see p. 12)?
8. Is there a build-up of dirt and wax toward the bottom of the piece and around the hinges?

Dressers
These are among the most saleable and sought-after items. Many bases retain their original rack. The base may be a floor-standing cupboard, a cupboard raised on legs and open below, or a potboard type (see pp. 120-21).
* As well as oak, some 18thC dressers are found in other country woods such as fruitwoods, or pine; yew wood examples are highly desirable.

Quality features
This dresser has some features that enhance its desirability:
* the architectural form of the

front shows a degree of sophistication that suggests the piece was made for a country house rather than a cottage
* the back is panelled. On simpler dressers the back will be made of rough planks nailed to the piece.

Note
The rules that apply to 18thC furniture in mahogany and satinwood do not apply as strictly to 18thC oak furniture, which was still made using traditional methods; thus, for example, the dovetails on an 18thC oak piece will be relatively thick for their date.

The interior

The cupboards are fitted with bearers for shelves, invariably put in at a later date.

* The insides of the doors should be unpolished and of a uniform colour, with no replacements. Fielded panels, such as those of this dresser, were popular on 18thC oak furniture. The panels were usually made from at least two pieces of wood, which may have opened up slightly with shrinkage (see p. 24).

The top

Typically, the top of this piece is made up of three boards which have opened up slightly. The small triangular split between the back and centre boards was caused by the nail used to secure the top when it became loose. Such splits can easily be repaired if an unblemished surface is preferred. The back edge has dark shading where it has not been polished as much as other areas. Similarly, the sides are likely to be darker than the top, which receives more light.

The handles

Although the handles are old, they are not original to the piece. The large plugged holes once held Victorian wooden knobs. There are also three holes around the keyhole escutcheon where another escutcheon plate was once secured.

* Dresser locks are often replacements or later additions. It is not uncommon for only one drawer to have had a lock originally.

Reproductions

Oak furniture of the 17thC tends to be darker than that of the 18thC. When 17th and 18thC styles were revived during the 19thC, a lighter, less figured oak was used, but often stained very dark, making the furniture almost black, in contrast to the natural richness of earlier pieces. This darker finish is currently not popular.

DRESSERS WITH RACKS

*An 18thC Montgomeryshire oak dresser with original rack
c.1720; ht 74in/188cm; wdth 77¹/₂in/197cm; value range B-E*

Identification checklist for early 18thC dressers
1. Is the piece oak? (Elm and yew were also used
occasionally.)
2. Are the drawers fairly crudely dovetailed or held
together with hand-made nails?
3. Is the piece of joined construction?
4. Has it built up a fine patina, and is this consistent top
and bottom?
5. Does the rack belong with the dresser base (see facing
page)?
6. Do the colour and construction of any drawers in the
top section match those of any in the lower section?

Dressers with racks
Some dressers were made with
racks for extra storage and display
space. These were made during
the same period as dressers
without racks (see pp. 118-19).
From the late 18thC the racks
occasionally incorporate tall
shallow side cupboards.

Regional variations
There are many stylistic
differences depending on where
the dresser was made. Many come
from Wales. Montgomeries, from
mid-Wales, usually have
exaggerated moulded tops and
though broad, are seldom tall.
120

They invariably have four front
legs and a wavy frieze. This
example also has turned back
legs, a desirable feature indicative
of quality.

Alterations
Dresser bases have sometimes
been reduced in width, usually
from a three-drawer to a two-
drawer piece. Compare the two
ends: if an alteration has been
made there will be signs of one
end having been cut and
remoulded. If the overall piece
looks ill-proportioned, the
rack may have been reduced in
height.

Legs
Some Montgomeryshire dressers have square legs. Dressers from the West Midlands often have cabriole legs.

"Marriages"
Dressers that retain their original rack command a premium, as many racks and dressers found today have been "married". It is usually fairly easy to tell whether a marriage has occurred, by examining the type and surface of the timber, which should be the same on both parts. Any carving or other decoration should also correspond on both parts.

Authenticity
The outline of the rack should be visible on the surface of the base when the rack is moved slightly. If the rack has "toes" that slot or tenon into the surface, the marks made by the toes should also be visible. In this case, a groove has been cut into the base (see *below*) to accommodate the toes of the rack and make it fit snugly. Other racks may screw into the base.
* Some racks are without boards at the back, and are fixed to the wall.

Sign of authenticity
Detail showing the base with the rack removed and the groove for the toes exposed. The outline of the rack is also clearly visible.

Drawers
Dressers on open bases usually have three drawers or, more rarely, four. If there are only two, this is a strong indication that the base may have been reduced in width (see **Alterations**).
Check that all the drawers match each other in terms of patina, type of dovetail and so on. There should not be any replacement drawers, and preferably no replacement parts, such as liners. On provincial pieces of this date the runners on which the drawers move are fixed to the carcass and slot into channels in the side of the drawer.
* Cabriole leg dressers, which date from c.1730, often have crossbanding around the drawers, usually in mahogany. Some dressers, especially later examples, also incorporate mahogany mouldings.

Handles
Marks on the drawer front indicate where the original handles (probably brass or wooden) have been. The current handles are Victorian.
* Fruitwood or yewwood knobs are not uncommon on oak dressers.

This detail from the back of one of the drawers shows where the previous handles have been fixed: one hole is plugged and not in use and the other was clearly not made by the current handle.

Potboard bases
The potboard at the base of the dresser should be original. It should match the rest of the piece in type of wood and grain, although it may well be dirtier than other surfaces, as it will not have received as much light or polish. For the same reasons, it may be paler in tone at the front than at the back.

GATELEG TABLES

A 17thC English oak gateleg table
c.1670-80; ht 28-in/72cm, lgth 60in/155.5cm, wdth (fully extended) 48in/122cm
value range B-F

Identification checklist for late 17th and 18thC gateleg tables
1. Is the table oak and in the solid?
2. Are the turned legs decorated with baluster twists or bobbins?
3. Do the surfaces have a good colour and patina?
4. Are the pegs hand-made (see p. 12)?
5. Are the drawers roughly constructed, perhaps with nails, and with chunky dovetails?
6. Do the feet exhibit signs of wear, especially those of the gates?
7. Are there marks on the underside of the table top where the gate has moved back and forth?

Gateleg tables
Most gateleg tables found today date from the late 17th and 18thC. They were made in all sizes, from those with flaps supported by single "gates" to very large examples needing two gates to support each flap. The changing style of leg is the best guide to dating (see pp. 110-13).

Note
* Although most gateleg tables are in oak, examples exist in walnut and other country woods. American gateleg tables are usually cherry, pine or walnut.
* The central bed or section may be made up of one, two or sometimes three planks. Two have been used in this example.

Drawers

The table has a single fitted drawer. Larger tables often have two drawers, although many gatelegs, whatever their size, have none. Drawers are often missing or replaced. This is not as serious as with, say, a chest or bureau, and most collectors would regard a missing or replacement drawer as acceptable in this context.

Authenticity

The outline of the arc made by the gateleg as it moves back and forth when the table is open and closed is visible on the underside of the table top, and confirms that the leg belongs with the top.

Feet and legs

The feet of gateleg tables often show signs of wear, especially those of the gate itself, which is dragged across the floor to support the flaps, and then pulled back to the central bed when the flaps are let down. Often, worn feet have been cut down or even replaced altogether. As the foot and leg were originally turned from one piece, if a repair has been made there will be a telltale joint and a break in the grain direction. This type of repair will adversely affect the value, but by how much will depend upon the amount and quality of the restoration.

Flaps

The flaps may be tipped at the edges, that is, finished off with separate pieces of timber joined to the flap by dowelling and glue. Replaced tips, which are quite common, can be detected by comparing the colour of the flaps with the colour around the edges. This may be done more easily from the underside. Replaced tips do reduce the value.

* One or both of the flaps may be darker than the central bed of the table if the table was frequently used either without the flaps raised or with only one flap: the bed will have faded, having been exposed longer to light.

Rule joints

The flaps hang from the main bed of the table by means of rule joints and iron hinges. This is the neatest kind of joint and an invariable sign of quality. (The more usual type of joint has an exposed hinge.)

Value points

* Assuming comparable quality, the larger the table, the more expensive it will be.
* Turned stretchers are generally more desirable than those that are simply moulded.

DROP-LEAF TABLES

*An English George II-period mahogany drop-leaf dining table
c.1740; ht 28¹/₂in/72cm; max. wdth 42in/106.5cm; max lgth 47in/120.5cm;
value range C–F (depending on size)*

Identification checklist for 18thC drop-leaf tables
1. Is the table either mahogany or Virginia walnut?
2. Has it been made in the solid?
3. Is the whole design very simple, relying on the quality and colour of the timber?
4. Is the table of oval shape?
5. Does it have a gateleg action that supports the flaps?
6. Do the legs terminate in pad or claw-and-ball feet?
7. Is the top plain, without inlay or other decoration?
8. Is the central section of the top made from one piece of wood?
9. Is the edge finished off with thumb moulding?
10. Does the table have a shaped frieze?

Drop-leaf tables
The drop-leaf table is a refined successor to the earlier oak gateleg table (see pp. 122–3), and the flaps are supported in the same way, with a gateleg action. Most are in Virginia walnut or mahogany. These tables were particularly popular during the George II period. They were made in a range of sizes, and in occasional as well as dining form. They are more comfortable to sit at than gateleg tables as they have fewer legs and no stretchers; also, the overhang of the top is greater. The example *above* is a very small dining table which seats four or six people. At this size drop-leaf tables are quite readily available and relatively modest in price, but larger ones are disproportionately more expensive. They sometimes have a drawer in the central bed or section. Drop-leaf tables are invariably in the solid and not veneered. Examples with carved legs (which usually terminate in claw-and-ball or pad feet) are generally more valuable than those with no carving. Drop-leaf tables are not known to have been faked. In the United States the drop-leaf table was the main form of dining table until the 18thC and both English and American examples are highly sought after.

Legs and feet
The turned leg terminating in a pad foot is the most common type on these tables, although grander examples might have cabrioles, the very finest of which have carved decoration. Legs and feet are the most vulnerable part of these tables and should therefore be examined carefully for signs of damage, replacement or wear. Pad feet are often repaired. The legs and feet of this table have acquired an attractive patination. They are undamaged but show the expected knocks and bangs, especially toward the bottom.

The top
The tops of drop-leaf tables are rarely inlaid or crossbanded. If you come across one that has been decorated in this way, the decoration is almost certain to have been done at a later date. Perhaps because drop-leaf tables tend not to be decorated, the quality of the timber is usually high and of good colour, as it is in this example, which is also in good condition, with no splits. At this small size the flaps should be made in one piece, but on larger examples more than one plank may have been used. The central section or "bed" is usually made up of one piece, which is relatively narrow, even on large examples. Always compare the colour of the pieces that make up the top to check that there are no replacements. Flaps meet by means of a rule hinge joint. Check that the edges of the flaps have not been "tipped": the flaps, being long grain, have occasionally been damaged and the outer edges are sometimes replaced.

Authenticity
The underside of the top should be unpolished and of an even colour. The edge will be darker or "shadowed" where it has been handled and acquired a different patination. If the shadowing does not continue all the way round, it may be that the top has been reshaped. As well as its even colour, untouched surface and continuous dark edge, another sign of authenticity here is the mark made on the underside of the table by the gateleg swinging across it.

Carved drop-leaf tables
This more elaborate drop-leaf table is also from the mid-18thC and has the same basic form as the plainer example opposite, but the carving indicates that in its day this was a high-fashion piece. The timber – Virginia walnut – has faded to a warm golden colour compatible with a table of this age. The carved beads and acanthus leaves are typical of the early to mid-18thC, as are the claw-and-ball feet. A table of this quality would fetch two or three times the price of a plain example of similar size.

PEDESTAL DINING TABLES

*A late 18thC English mahogany pedestal dining table
c.1790; ht 29in/73.5cm, wdth with one leaf (not shown) 47in/119.5cm; value range B–D*

Identification checklist for late 18thC pedestal dining tables

1. Is the table mahogany?
2. Does it have a gun barrel pedestal stem?
3. Do the pedestals have splayed legs?
4. Does the table top have a reeded edge?
5. Are the casters plain?
6. Do any leaves belong with the table?

Pedestal dining tables
Dining tables with pedestal bases were first seen in England from the mid-18thC; a few were made in the United States in the early 19thC. They range from those with two pedestals up to those with four. Examples with two pedestals are the most common variety and, although expensive if original, are still more affordable than the type with three or four. The price is governed by the number of pedestals — the three-pedestal type may fetch more than double the price of one with two pedestals — and by how original the table is (see opposite), as well as by the colour, figuring and elegance. The gun-barrel pedestal of the table, *above*, is the most desirable type. Another good feature of this table is the well-figured top, now faded to a particularly pleasant colour. The
126

two sections have been nicely matched up. Chippendale-period tables are characterized by their strength of design; those from the late 18thC by their elegance, exemplified by that shown *above*; 19thC examples (see facing page) became heavier and more ornate as the century progressed.

Leaves
Three-pedestal tables have two leaves; those with four pedestals have three. The extra leaves fit between the main leaves when the top is opened and are held in place with locating lugs and brass clips that slot in from the sides. They may also be supported by bearers that slot in underneath, or by arms that pivot out. Leaves are prone to warping especially those not supported by bearers: put them all in the table and check they are not bowed.

Marriages

Pedestal tables are sometimes made up by reshaping a Victorian top and putting it onto an earlier style pedestal base, not necessarily to deceive, but for aesthetic reasons: large Victorian dining tables usually have very heavy bulbous turned legs and are less desirable than earlier pedestal tables (although the timber is generally very good). Many people find these made-up tables acceptable, as they should be considerably less expensive than an authentic pedestal table. A made-up table may be detected by the following signs:

* a new pedestal will not show the expected signs of wear, especially at the edges, which are particularly vulnerable
* the casters may not show appropriate knocks and signs of wear: 18thC casters are brass, which is soft and therefore vulnerable; reproduction casters are usually steel
* both the bearers and the blocks on top of the pedestals, if newly made up, will not display the natural signs of wear that will be evident on 18thC blocks and bearers
* the underside of the table top may show evidence of other screw holes or marks made by the bearers of the original table.

Note

Pedestal tables are virtually always made in the solid – usually in mahogany – and the tops are therefore without crossbanding. Crossbanded tops are indicative of reproductions or decoration added at a later date.

Replaced leaves

Leaves are often replaced: the colour of the timber and grain of each one should match. They are best examined from the underside as the fixed part of the top may be more faded than the leaves. Leaves should be of the same thickness as the top. A matched leaf is unlikely to have been exactly the same width as the table, and was probably trimmed to the correct width; any reeding or moulding will have been freshly cut and may show signs of artificial distressing. Matched leaves are acceptable but should be reflected in the price.

Later pedestal tables

By the William IV period when this table was made, bases had become very heavy and designs robust. However, some examples are nevertheless quite attractive, as this one is, and the better ones are now much more sought-after than they used to be. Prices are rising, so they still currently represent good value.

BREAKFAST TABLES

An early 19thC English rosewood breakfast table
c.1815; ht 28in/71cm; dia 48in/122cm; value range C-F

Identification checklist for early 19thC breakfast tables
1. Is the table veneered, either in rosewood or mahogany?
2. Are the stem and feet turned in beech and stained to simulate rosewood?
3. Is the table supported by a central pedestal on a platform base?
4. Is the platform base either 3- or 4-cornered?
5. Does the table have boldly carved feet supporting the platform?
6. Does the table top have a frieze?
7. Is the top circular or rectangular?
8. Does the top belong with the base (see *below*)?

Breakfast tables

Most 18thC breakfast tables are rectangular with rounded corners; round and oval examples from this period are rare, although from the early 19thC round examples on a pedestal or platform base are as plentiful as rectangular ones. They were made in considerable numbers during the early 19thC. The finest examples incorporate cross-banded decoration, like that of the table shown opposite, and may have cast gilt metal feet, intricate brass line inlay, or gilt metal moulding around the base of the frieze. The example *above* would have been considered fairly basic in its day – it is of good quality but lacks any outstanding decorative details. Size also varies: large examples, to seat 8 or more, are rarer and considerably more expensive than smaller examples of equal quality.

128

Authenticity

Tilt the top from the base and examine the block: this should show signs of where the top has rested on it over the years. Similarly, the outline of the block, however faint, should be visible on the underside of the table top.

Alterations

Late 18thC round and oval breakfast tables are more sought after than rectangular examples. As a result, many plain rectangular-topped tables have been "improved" by having their tops reshaped. Indications that this has happened include:
* a poorly shaped oval outline
* few signs of wear on the "new" edges of the top
* bearers that have been reduced to accommodate the smaller top
* the top appearing too small for the base.

The top

The top of the table is veneered in five narrowish strips which highlight the attractive figuring of the rosewood (rosewood is rarely available in wide leaves). The surface exhibits the kind of small scratches and marks that are to be expected from a table of this age.

* Although these tables are most commonly found in rosewood or mahogany, some, which show a Continental influence, are veneered in pale woods such as bird's-eye maple.

Column and base

The column and carved feet are in solid rosewood – an unusual sign of quality. A cheaper alternative would be the use of beech stained to resemble rosewood (*faux* rosewood). An attractive feature is the way the veneers on the base echo those of the table top.

The precise form of the pedestal base is an aid to dating: in the Sheraton period the splayed legs appeared to simply and elegantly flow from the central column. During the Regency, sabre legs appeared to project from the sides of the column. The example on the previous page has a tricorn platform base, a type introduced during the early 19thC, mostly for high fashion pieces and in common use by 1820. The alternative at this period would be a four-cornered platform base or a pedestal (see *below*).

Pedestal breakfast tables

This splendid example of a small mahogany breakfast table, c.1800, has a well-figured top which has faded to a particularly fine colour. It is without a frieze – a feature not introduced until the early 19thC. The table has a turned pedestal (the alternative at this period to the platform base) with reeded legs terminating in plain toe caps. The decoration around the edge of the table is indicative of the quality of the piece, consisting of a wide band of coromandel cross-banding, between narrower bands of satinwood, all laid in short sections to follow the angles of the table.

* The bearers, whose edges are visible beneath the table top, are part of the basic structure and add stability and prevent warping.

129

D-ENDED DINING TABLES

A late 18thC English mahogany D-ended dining table
c.1775; wdth 48in/122cm, ht 28in/71cm, lgth 128in/325cm (fully extended); value range B-D

Identification checklist for late 18thC D-ended dining tables
1. Is the table mahogany?
2. Is the table top solid with a veneered frieze?
3. Are the legs slightly tapered?
4. Are the legs made from the solid?
5. Does the table have all its original leaves?
6. Is the table in good condition – a particularly important factor with this type of furniture (see facing page)?

D-ended dining tables
D-ended dining tables were first seen c.1760. Most are quite plain, the decorative features being restricted to the moulding of the square leg, or, in later examples, the turning or fluting, any shaping of the frieze and any moulding of the edges. They are versatile tables and can usually be used in a number of ways: typically, the example shown here has two D-ends, two leaves and a central section; the D-ends can be used together to make a small dining table, or be used with one leaf to make a table to seat eight, or with more leaves to accommodate twelve. The central section has a gateleg action that supports the leaves. The D-ends have fixed legs.

D-ended tables are steadier than those with pedestals, but are considerably less expensive, as

the legs tend to get in the way. The frieze of some D-ended tables may also make the table uncomfortable to sit at.

Later dining tables
In the early 19thC, this type of table gave way to extending dining tables, which tend to have turned legs. The "D" end was generally dropped in favour of ends of rectangular shape with rounded corners and with the inner legs being set in, making the table more comfortable to sit at. Various patented devices were introduced to open and close the table, but by the Victorian era the method had been somewhat standardized and large extending dining tables were opened and closed by means of a cranking handle. Some large reproductions are veneered and cross-banded, as the originals would not have been.

130

Flap mechanism
The use of steel hinges, *above*, that detach by means of an ingenious mechanism, allow the flaps to be removed altogether when not in use, rather than having to hang down at the side of the table. When in use the flaps clip in place (see *below left*).

Leaves
The table has all its original leaves. It is possible to determine this by comparing them for colour and grain match.
* Even genuine leaves may not all be the same colour, as they may not all have been used to the same degree. One leaf may hardly have been used and so will appear much darker, not having been exposed to the light and sun. However, the undersides of matching leaves should correspond, as should the brass clips on the underside which are used to hold the leaves together tightly. It is also advisable to compare the sides of the leaves, not only for colour, but to check that they are of corresponding thickness.
* Look for marks caused by the action of the gates on the underside of the table top. However, there should be no signs of any marks under the D-ends, and no unaccountable screw holes that might suggest the top has been made up from another piece of furniture.
* The hinges underneath the table should be rusty and well bedded-in and look as if they have always been there – a good sign of authenticity.

Legs
The shaped lappets at the top of the legs are a decorative feature particularly associated with furniture of the Chippendale period.

Toward the end of the 18thC legs generally became lighter and tapered, perhaps terminating in a spade foot. Later dining tables sometimes have a little decorative inlay, such as stringing, around the corners of the legs, on the edges of the table top and around the frieze.
* The outer edges of the legs will show more signs of damage than the inner surfaces. Check that the timber of the legs all corresponds, as replacements sometimes occur, and should be reflected in the price.
* Sit at the table to check that the legs are not too bulky nor the frieze too deep for comfort.

Condition
Condition is particularly relevant to the price. This table has survived very well, perhaps because it was made as a high-quality piece and has therefore always been well cared-for. It has no significant scratches, and no sign of splits or warping. The surface is in excellent condition – although tops can be repolished successfully, it is usually a time-consuming and costly operation.

SERVING TABLES

An English Sheraton-period mahogany serving table
c.1790; ht 33³/₄in/85.5, wdth 71¹/₂in/181.5cm, max dpth 24in/61cm; value range A-C

Identification checklist for late 18thC serving tables
1. Is the piece mahogany?
2. Is it of elegant and slender proportions?
3. Is it serpentine-, bow- or straight-fronted?
4. Are the legs slender, square and tapering, possibly with anklets toward the feet, or spade feet?
5. Does the table have one long central frieze drawer (possibly "divided" by false drawer fronts)?
6. Is there any decorative inlay or cross-banding?

Serving tables
Serving tables, the forerunners of sideboards, were introduced during the Chippendale period. Although designed for the dining room, they are also much used today in drawing rooms. The earliest examples were usually in the solid (with a veneered top) and in mahogany, that being the only timber available in large enough planks. The serving table shown, *above*, dates from the late 18thC, when styles were lighter and made greater use of decorative veneers. Some were designed to stand between pedestals with urns on top, the pedestals and table being made as a set. As they were usually intended for the important houses of the day, they are often of very large proportions. The example shown above is particularly desirable, not only because of its attractive, elegantly shaped serpentine front, but because it is

also only 24in/61cm deep (see **Alterations**). Most serving tables are rectangular; later examples often have a break-front; others, from the early 19thC are bow-fronted and often grandly decorative, with lion's monopodia legs and heavily carved feet.

Signs of quality
The serving table *above* is one of the finest of its type, and its desirability is enhanced by several features:
* serpentine form
* top-quality mahogany veneer, which is beautifully figured and rich in colour
* cross banding and stringing on the drawers, sides, top and the edges of the legs, with the characteristic oval paterae inlaid at the top of the legs
* drawers oak- rather than pine-lined
* decoration extended to the sides of the piece.

Alterations

Serving tables have not traditionally been prone to fakery, perhaps because until recently they were not in great demand and consequently were relatively inexpensive. However, because they tend to be very deep they are sometimes reduced in depth to increase their saleability. This necessitates cutting and remaking the drawers, a process that involves remaking the whole back section, including reworking the tenons and bearers. It is possible to detect a serving table that has been reduced in depth through the following clues:

* the proportions of the overall piece may look wrong
* where the back and veneers have been cut, the surface will probably look relatively fresh, and the edge may be too sharp, lacking the expected signs of wear and discoloration. Internal examination of the back of the piece may also reveal fresh working
* decorative stringing or cross banding may reveal signs of having been cut and remitred
* the drawers will have been cut and re-jointed
* the back legs will show signs of disturbance at the joints where they have been replaced.
(See also pp. 134-5.)

The handles and escutcheon

Although the fittings are stylistically correct for the period, on examining the wood around them, it is apparent that the piece originally had handles and an escutcheon of a different size and shape: their outlines are still faintly visible. Unused fixing holes will be apparent on the back of the drawers.

Later serving tables

This George IV serving table aptly shows the difference between the stylistically restrained serving tables of the 18thC and the more imposing type of furniture made in the 19thC for the burgeoning middle classes. Serving tables of the 19thC are often large and invariably in mahogany. They are frequently found with a bowed breakfront form and four front legs. As high-fashion items, quality is usually high. This example, in common with many later serving tables, has no drawers.

A late 18thC English mahogany sideboard
c.1790; max ht 47in/120cm, wdth 65¹/₂in/167cm, dpth 26in/67.5cm; value range B-D

Identification checklist for 18thC sideboards
1. Is the sideboard mahogany?
2. Is it veneered?
3. Does it have decorative inlays, crossbanding or stringing?
4. Does it have six square tapering legs – four at the front and two at the back, each made in one piece (see Leg replacements on facing page)?
5. Do the legs terminate in spade feet?
6. Are the sides of the sideboard quite plain, with the decoration being confined to the top and/or front?
7. Is is bow- or serpentine-fronted?

18thC sideboards
Sideboards were introduced into England in 1775. The one shown *above* has several typical late 18thC features:
* oval/circular inlaid panels/motifs
* brass curtain rail
* square tapering legs terminating in spade feet
* ring handles with embossed backplates
* inlaid and crossbanded decoration
* cellaret drawer
* bow-fronted form. Straight-fronted examples also exist.
The serpentine form is generally considered the most desirable of all.

Signs of quality
The sideboard *above* has a number of quality features:
* attractive decoration, including mahogany and kingwood banding and boxwood and ebonized stringing
* figured quality veneers
* spade rather than plain feet.

Reproductions and copies
Some Edwardian copies incorporate fine-quality inlaid marquetry and are generally of high quality and very sought after today. However, those Edwardian and later reproductions made with cheaper veneers should be avoided.

Cupboard-space
A nice feature is the additional cupboard space provided beneath the central arch, enclosed by a tambour-fronted sliding door. The whole cupboard pulls forward, and slides back when not in use.

Alterations
Large sideboards are particularly prone to structural alteration, which may take one of two forms.

1. Reduction in depth
Although this sideboard is a saleable size, some 18thC examples are very large and many have a deep overhang at the back to allow for the deep skirtings and dado rails of 18thC houses. This overhang is sometimes removed to make the piece shallower. In many cases this is acceptable provided that some overhang remains. As such alterations have usually taken place in the last 30 or 40 years the back edge will look freshly cut and perhaps artificially distressed, and the corners will not yet have rounded with age. The depth may be further reduced by remaking the drawers so that they are shallower (see p. 133). Internally, there will probably be signs of reworking at the back of the piece.

2. Leg replacements
Some apparently 18thC sideboards may in fact date from the early 19thC, when the less fashionable ring-turned legs were used. These often get cut off below the drawer level and are replaced with 18thC-style square tapering legs. Such deception is relatively easy to detect upon close inspection of the timber used in the upper and lower parts of the leg: as the whole leg is usually made from one piece of timber, look to see if there is a joint, indicative of a re-make. This may be easier to see from the back, as a joint at the front could be concealed by decorative stringing. A non-match in colour and grain of timber would also indicate an alteration.

Condition
Sideboards come in for more usage than many other types of furniture and a degree of wear is to be expected from even the finest pieces. Replaced stringing or minor blemishes should not deter the prospective purchaser.

Cellaret drawer
Typically for an 18thC sideboard, one of the deep drawers pulls out to reveal a lead-lined cellaret to hold wine bottles. Such linings are often in a poor state of repair and may need restoration. The other drawer has a plain interior.

19THC SIDEBOARDS

An early 19thC English mahogany pedestal sideboard
c.1815; ht 43¹/2in/109cm, wdth 90¹/2in/230cm; value range D-F

Identification checklist for early 19thC sideboards
1. Is the sideboard mahogany?
2. Is it high quality – for example, does it show signs of attention to detail?
3. Does it have turned feet?
4. Has it been constructed in several sections, perhaps three (see facing page)?
5. Has it been inlaid or applied with other decorative details?
6. Are the handles original?

19thC sideboards
The early 19thC saw a total innovation design-wise – the sideboards on legs of the 18thC (see pp. 134-5), were at least in part superseded by sideboards on pedestals, many of which were made with matching cellarets, although it is very unusual to find sideboards with their original cellarets. Until very recently sideboards of the type shown *above* have been very unsaleable despite the fact that they are invariably of fine quality and in their day were high fashion pieces. During the Victorian period sideboards were made in greater numbers and quality was variable (see facing page).
136

Value
Because of their recent unsaleability 19thC pedestal sideboards are still remarkably inexpensive considering their high quality, but they have started to become popular and prices are bound to rise.

It is not an area that is fraught with fakes and marriages, and copies were not made once the pieces fell from fashion at the end of the Regency period. The main buying criteria are, of course, size, and also quality – for example, is the wood of high quality, what kind of fittings do the cupboards have, and what kind of decorative details are there, if any?

Handles
The handles are contemporary with the piece but are not the originals: there are marks on the drawer front where another handle has swung against it, and also the faint outline of another handle.

Condition
As sideboard doors are often fairly broad they should be inspected for signs of splitting, which, if deep or extensive, will certainly be detrimental to value.

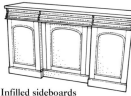

Infilled sideboards
In the Victorian period the empty area between the pedestals was quite often infilled to provide extra storage space, see *above*. This type was produced in large numbers. They vary in quality from simply constructed examples to quite fantastic ones. Those that have carved decoration and are surmounted by a large mirror tend to be of very fine quality.

Decoration
The quality of the sideboard can be seen in the very fine flamed veneers used and the coromandel and rosewood bandings and mouldings around the door frames. The top of the central section and the pedestals are also cross-banded in rosewood. The mitred crossbanding in zebrawood is particularly indicative of quality.

Construction
Pedestal sideboards are made in three sections: the central section simply fits between the cupboards and is usually screwed in and held with locating lugs. The cupboards may be fitted – for example, one may have a shelf and a deep drawer, and the other may have two shelves, or perhaps be fitted with a cellaret. As furniture designed to stand against a wall, the back is invariably left unfinished, even on pieces of the highest quality.

Late-Victorian and Edwardian sideboards
These were often modelled on late 18thC styles, especially on those with inlaid decoration. This harewood and marquetry example of c.1875 is of exaggerated design: it would be unusual to find an 18thC sideboard so profusely decorated.

WINE COOLERS

An early 19thC English sarcophagus-shaped mahogany wine cooler c.1810; ht 24in/61cm; value range D-E.

Identification checklist for early 19thC wine coolers
1. Is the wine cooler mahogany?
2. Is it sarcophagus-shaped?
3. Does it have lion's-mask handles?
4. Does it have hairy lion's-paw feet?
5. Does it have ebonized mouldings and black line inlay?
6. Does it have nulled mouldings?

Wine coolers and cellarets
Cellarets are used for the short term storing of wine, wine coolers for cooling bottles immediately before consumption. Wine coolers have traditionally been more sought after than cellarets and fetch higher prices, perhaps because they are often used as jardinières.

Cellarets and wine coolers were introduced in England around the middle of the 18thC. They were not much favoured in the United States. The stands are usually made separately from the top. They are mostly in mahogany, but found in other woods, such as satinwood and walnut. In the 18thC many were on raised legs, with carrying handles and brass banding. Victorian examples are often elaborately carved, with grapes and other motifs.

138

The very fine example *above* is in the manner of Gillows – a leading English maker of the Regency period. Originally it would have been designed in conjunction with a pedestal sideboard or serving table. The design is innovative in that it is not raised on a tall stand. However, it has several typical early 19thC features:
* sarcophagus shape
* applied lion's-mask and ring handles
* ebonized mouldings and inlay (black line inlay was fashionable after Nelson, as were stringing and black mouldings)
* hairy lion's-paw feet in finely cast gilt metal
* nulling at the top of the legs and on the top itself
* diamond-shaped inlaid escutcheons.

The lining

The wine cooler retains its original lead lining, which has all the reassuring knocks, scratches and signs of wear.

* Although the hinges have a stop mechanism to keep the lid open without it having to be held – a typical Georgian feature also found on caddies and box furniture – it is advisable not to leave the lid open unsupported. Be similarly wary of lifting a piece by its carrying handles as these are often more decorative than functional.

Marriages

This cellaret from the George III period is characterized by its octagonal form and three brass bands. The base is not original to the top – the legs are rather too straight, giving the piece a slightly top-heavy appearance.

The underside

The underside is as to be expected: it has a dry, undisturbed look, with no sign of fresh timber or alterations. The casters are original and appropriately worn for their age.

Authenticity

A number of cellarets and wine coolers are found on replacement stands. Separate the two parts: any marks or signs of wear on the underside of the top should correspond with those on the top of the base. The colour of the wood, and any decorative details, should match. Provided that the base is well made, replacements are acceptable but should be allowed for in the price.

18thC wine coolers

This is a standard lead-lined 18thC wine cooler, c.1770, of a type often found with a tap or plug on the bottom to drain off melted ice. Some examples are fitted with pierced spandrels.

Condition

Wine coolers, like barrels, are made in small sections, glued and bound by brass bands. The glue in time dries out causing the piece to become rickety; if this has happened it may have to be dismantled and reassembled. The bands sometimes drop off. Compare them for colour, wear and patina: original bands will be of a yellowish brass, patinated, and with softened edges.

WRITING FURNITURE

Throughout the 16thC most householders kept papers in chests. Letters or documents were written at a kind of small portable table-top desk in the form of a box with a hinged sloping top. These were in oak and either carved or inlaid.

During the first half of the 17thC these portable desks were still the only form of furniture in England specifically designed for writing. After the Restoration they began to be made with a stand, and a drawer and compartments were also added.

The first item of French and Italian writing furniture is the *escritoire*, which dates from the early 16thC and consists of a case of drawers and compartments on a stand, enclosed by a front that lets down to provide a writing surface. The *escritoire* enjoyed only a brief period of popularity in England, during the late 17thC and early 18thC. Being high-fashion pieces in their day, *escritories* are mainly found veneered in walnut and occasionally with seaweed or marquetry decoration. Commercially, those of English origin have never been as popular as say, the more practical bureau, and this is reflected in the prices they fetch. Other Continental versions of the *escritoire* include the *vargueño*, a Spanish fall-front cabinet which was also popular on the west coast of the United States.

Good examples of English bureaux in veneered walnut are always much in demand, especially smaller ones. The earliest form of bureau evolved from the writing box and was made in two sections, the upper section with a hinged slope being placed on a case of drawers, with a moulding to conceal the joint. During the mid-17thC this developed into the one-section bureau, although the waist moulding was retained until the 1720s.

By the William and Mary period bureaux had become more sophisticated. Some had cabinets or bookcases placed on top. The earliest of these have veneered wood panels. Later, some had mirrored panel doors accompanied by pull-out candle slides. With the exception of provincial pieces, which continued to be made in oak, most late 17thC bureaux are in veneered walnut. A few have japanned and gilt chinoiserie decoration. The finest of these are among the most expensive items of English furniture.

Kneehole desks were introduced early in the 18thC and, although originally intended as dressing tables, were generally used as ladies' writing desks. They are made in one section and comprise a central recessed cupboard door with a single drawer above and two banks of three drawers either side. Kneehole desks continued to be made throughout the Chippendale period, usually in mahogany.

In the United States the bureau and bureau bookcase were popular from c.1700, based on English designs but with local characteristics, such as the "bonnet top" – an architecturally shaped top of more exaggerated form than its English equivalent. Later examples display Continental influences – for example, in the use of a block-front or bombé form (rarely found in English cabinet-making).

By the mid-18thC the bureau is usually made in mahogany and has an altogether less solid appearance. Any bookcase tops are now glazed, with slender astragals. The best examples have an interesting interior, perhaps with a central cupboard and pull-out slides (in addition to the usual drawers and pigeon-holes), an architectural pediment and an unusual astragal formation.

Pedestal desks, similar to kneehole desks but made in one section, first appeared in the mid-18thC and by the end of the century were firmly established; the finest examples are adorned with carved decoration.

Another new mid-18thC form was the secretaire or secretary bookcase, introduced during the 1750s as a variation of the bureau bookcase. The lower section comprises a deep pull-out secretaire drawer that opens to reveal a fitted interior. The drawer front is hinged and lets down to provide the writing surface. Beneath the secretaire drawer there are either three long drawers, or cupboards with sliding trays. Although chests-on-chests do not strictly fall into the category of writing furniture, some examples are occasionally fitted with a pull-out secretaire drawer and are primarily for use in the bedroom.

Much of the writing furniture made on the Continent of Europe during the mid-18thC is imposing in form and elaborately decorated both on the inside and on the outside.

In England during the last quarter of the 18thC the secretaire bookcase was preferred to the bureau bookcase. More emphasis was now placed on inlaid (as opposed to carved) decoration, especially oval-shaped motifs. Many have light Gothic glazing bars. The elegant writing table also continued to be popular during the last quarter of the 18thC, again in lighter, more elegant styles.

Several new designs were introduced by the turn of the century. These include the cylinder desk, the *bonheur du jour* – a ladies' writing desk – and the Carlton House desk, so called because the first one is said to have been designed for the bedroom of the Prince Regents' London residence, Carlton House. Other new forms were the writing table with end supports, and the davenport – a compact piece with a writing slope above a case of drawers or cabinet. These new designs remained popular into the Regency period in more elaborate and ornate versions and in some cases – for example, in that of the davenport – throughout the Victorian period as well.

In the United States the bureau bookcase remained popular well into the early 19thC, when many were found with the currently fashionable splay foot. Cylinder desks and secretaries on tall legs with open bases were also popular although the secretary bookcase had less appeal and enjoyed a briefer period of popularity.

BUREAUX

An English William and Mary/Queen Anne walnut bureau c.1700/10; wdth 33in/84cm; value range B-E.

Identification checklist for late 17th/early 18thC bureaux

1. Is the bureau oak, or walnut-veneered onto pine or oak?
2. Is it quarter-veneered (see below)?
3. Is there cross banding and/or feather banding around the top, fall, or drawer fronts?
4. Does the bureau have bun feet (or, more rarely at this period, bracket feet)?
5. Are the mouldings cross-grained?
6. Are the dovetails fairly chunky?
7. Are the lopers (the pull-out bearers that support the writing surface) fairly shallow – less than the depth of the top drawer?
8. Is the back made of a secondary wood?
9. Does the piece have a well?

Woods

In the United States until the mid-18thC, when mahogany became prevalent, Baltic pine and maple were used in addition to oak and walnut.

Size

Smaller bureaux – approx. 30in (76cm) wide – are generally considered more desirable than larger ones, especially those more than approx. 42in (107cm).

The veneer

The veneer of the bureau shown *above* is nicely figured. The fall and top are quartered; that is, made up of four pieces of veneer, book-matched to create a symmetrical design. The veneering and patterning on the drawer fronts are also matched. Feather banding, a typical Queen Anne feature (see p. 14), is inlaid into the fall, the top, and around the edges of the drawers.

Bureaux

In the 17thC bureaux were made in two parts – a bureau top and chest base, with a "waist" moulding to cover the joint. This moulding was retained even after bureaux began to be made in one piece at the beginning of the 18thC, but was finally dropped c.1720. The bureau shown here was made in one piece, but retains the waist moulding. From this period on designs varied very little, but the type of wood, handles and decoration will provide clues for dating.

Drawers

Drawers can either be oak-lined and the fronts veneered onto oak, as in the piece shown here, or pine could be used instead. However, pine tends to bow and thus pull drawer fronts out of shape. Provided that any warping is not too dramatic, it will not seriously affect the value.
Some bureaux have two short and three long drawers and no well. Others have one long top drawer instead of a well, two short drawers beneath that, and then two long drawers. Some mahogany bureaux have four long drawers. The type with three deep drawers only is not as desirable.

Interiors

The quality of the fitments and the amount of detail have a signficant bearing on price. Some bureaux are fitted with a concealed well, which can be reached only from the inside by pushing back the covering slide, as has been done here, to reveal a hollow section. The interior of this example is fairly simple. In addition to the well, the bureau has small pull-out "secret" slides (disguised as pilasters) on either side of the central cupboard.

Handles

The handles, though stylistically correct, are replacements: slight marks made by other handles are evident on the drawer front. It is particularly important to check for such signs in cases like this one, where the present handles have been there long enough to acquire naturally a patina and build-up of dirt and wax.

Bun feet

Bun feet are characteristic of the late 17th and early 18thC. Around 90% of those found today are not original. Those of this bureau are replacements, which have been subtly distressed to blend in with the piece. Toward the mid-18thC many bun feet were replaced by the newly popular bracket feet; thus even where a piece now has bracket feet, it may belong to the earlier, bun-foot period: remove the lower drawer and look for marks similar to those shown in the detail *above*, of where a bun foot may originally have been tenoned into the baseboard.

Later, mahogany bureaux

The Chippendale period was the heyday of the mahogany bureau, made from c.1730. Mahogany bureaux differ in several ways from earlier, walnut bureaux:
* they have bracket feet
* they usually have swan-neck brass handles with shaped backplates (see pp. 26-7)
* lopers are deeper, usually the length of the top drawer
* they were made in the solid, although veneered examples also exist
* they seldom have a waist moulding
* the moulding along the base is straight-grained in full-length pieces, whereas on earlier bureaux it is cross-grained in short pieces (see p. 14).

143

BUREAU BOOKCASES

*An English George III-period mahogany bureau bookcase
c.1775; ht 84¹/₄in/214.5cm; wdth 40in/101.5cm; value range A-D*

Identification checklist for late 18thC bureau bookcases
1. Is the piece mahogany?
2. Does it have bracket feet?
3. Does it have an arcaded pear-drop cornice or other decorative details?
4. Is there cock beading around the drawers?
5. Are the lopers the depth of the top drawer?
6. Do the drawers match each other in style of construction?
7. Are the dovetails relatively fine?
8. Do the sections belong together (see p. 31)?
9. Is the glazing original (see p. 161)?

Bureau bookcases
All the major styles of bureau were also made in bureau-bookcase form from c.1690, in styles that matched other furniture of the period. They were invariably constructed in two pieces, the bookcase resting within the moulding on the top of the bureau, which is left unfinished, and held in place by screws. American bureau bookcases were based on English designs but with Continental influences, such as the *bombé* form.

Signs of quality
The bureau bookcase *above* has several desirable features:
* the veneers of the drawers have clearly come from the same batch, and have been nicely matched up so that the figuring runs evenly through
* interesting cornice
* well-fitted interior.

The interior
The attractively fitted interior adds considerably to the desirability of the piece. The central cupboard, highlighted with stringing and banding, draws the elements together visually and makes a refreshing change from the more conventional arrangement of a row of drawers surmounted by pigeon holes. The arcading at the top of the pigeon holes is also a nice feature. Sometimes such arcading pulls out as a shallow secret drawer.

* The semicircular mark to the left of the lock has been caused by the inner door swinging against the fall as it is closed – a reassuring sign of age and authenticity.

Falls
Falls are prone to splitting, especially in the hinge area; there is evidence on this example of slight cracks and minor splits which have been repaired. They are also prone to warping, being made of one relatively large piece of wood.
* There should be a lighter area on the carcass where the fall has rested against it, protecting it from the build-up of dirt and wax that will have occurred on unprotected surfaces.

Construction
Fixing holes are evident in the base of the bookcase. These should correspond with holes visible on the top of the bureau when the sections are separated.
* The backboards of the top half may be panelled, whereas those of the base may not be. This does not mean that the pieces do not belong together: usually only the back of the upper part is panelled, being visible (because of the glazing). However, if different woods have been used top and bottom, the piece should be regarded with caution.
* The shelves are adjustable, and inspection of these may reveal an alteration in size (see p. 161).

Handles
The style of the handles is a good guide to dating (see pp. 26-7) – but only if they are original to the piece. The handles on this bureau bookcase are stylistically correct for the period and there are no suspicious marks on the drawer fronts. However, an inspection on the reverse of the drawer reveals a large, central unused hole, probably where there was a Victorian wooden knob handle – the first replacement.

SECRETAIRE BOOKCASES

*A late 18thC English mahogany secretaire bookcase
c.1790; ht 80in/203cm, wdth 30in/76cm; value range B-D*

Identification checklist for late 18thC secretaire
bookcases
1. Is the piece mahogany?
2. Are the drawers finely dovetailed?
3. Does the piece have splayed bracket feet?
4. Does it have inlaid decoration in a contrasting wood?
5. Are the glazing bars correct for the period?
6. Are the shelves adjustable?
7. Are the drawer linings mahogany or "pencil" cedar?
8. If the handles are original, are they embossed, with an
oval or circular backplate?
9. Do the sections belong together (see facing page)?

Secretaire bookcases

The secretaire bookcase was first seen c.1750 and fulfils the same function as a bureau bookcase (see pp. 144-5). There are two types of secretaire bookcase: the most common type has a deep pull-out secretaire drawer with a row of three drawers below, as in the example shown *left*. The drawer front lowers to form the writing surface. A more unusual arrangement has a secretaire drawer with a pair of panelled cupboards below, fitted with sliding shelves or trays.
* Secretaire bookcases in satinwood command a premium.

Genuine or marriage?

Secretaire bookcases are more prone to being married than any other type of furniture. A genuine piece should have characteristics common to both sections, such as:
* matching decorative bandings on both parts. The banding around the base and drawers of the chest of this piece are reflected in the pediment
* matching wood used top and bottom. It is best to compare the sides of the pieces. Check the grain as well as the colour, as one section may have received more light than another and thus be more faded.

The top of the chest base should not be veneered as it is designed to be covered by the bookcase. If you are examining a secretaire bookcase and the base has a veneered top, the piece is probably a marriage (but bear in mind that with antique furniture there are always exceptions to the rule).

Construction

All secretaire bookcases are made in two sections (plus the pediment, which is usually screwed down). The top sits on the base and is held by two or four screws. The screw holes will be evident on the base of the cabinet and should correspond with holes on the top of the chest base. (The moulding between the cabinet and the chest base can be applied either to the bottom of the cabinet or, as in this piece, to the top of the chest.)

Pediments usually sit between locating blocks on the cornice and are fixed on with locating screws. When the pediment is removed the top of the bookcase will probably show shading where the pediment has sat over the years.

Authenticity

As with all two-part furniture, any marks caused by special features on one half should be reflected on the other half – for example, if the bookcase stands on shaped bearers fixed to the top of the chest, there should be marks on the underside of the bookcase, however subtle, showing where it has stood on the bearers. In this case, there are two sets of small holes, one set plugged, on the underside of the bookcase where it was screwed to the chest base. The first pair probably became too loose to hold the screws and had to be relocated slightly. On a genuine piece such as this, the chest top will have two corresponding pairs of holes.

Watch point

The bookcases are usually fitted with three or four adjustable shelves. The row of grooves for the shelves starts approximately 6in (15cm) from the base of the cabinet, and finishes 6in (15cm) from the top. If a shelf is so near the top or bottom of the bookcase as not to leave sufficient height for a book, this is a strong indication that the bookcase has been reduced in size.

Value point

Very large secretaire bookcases, over 8ft/24.3m tall and wider than 4ft/12.2m, fetch less than smaller ones.

Glazing

The glazing, which is secured to the glazing bars with putty, is original, and can be detected by its rippled surface. The earlier the glass the more ripples it will have.

An Empire-period mahogany escritoire
c.1825; max ht 62¹/₂in/159cm; wdth 31¹/₂in/80cm; value range C-E.

Identification checklist for early 19thC Continental *escritoires*

1. Is the *escritoire* mahogany?
2. Is it veneered?
3. Does it have brass inlay and/or ormolu mounts?
4. Is the top marbled?
5. Is the inside elaborately fitted?
6. Has the *escritoire* been made in one piece? (English *escritoires* are usually made in two sections.)
7. Does it have slender turned feet?
8. Are the handles and other brasswork original?

Escritoires
Escritoires – cabinets with a hinged front which provides a writing surface, and a fitted interior – enjoyed only a brief period of popularity in England, 148

between the late 17th and early 18thC. However, they were popular on the Continent throughout the 18thC and into the 19thC. The example *above* is particularly fine.

Continental features

The late 18th and early 19thC in France was a period of furniture design which shows a degree of restraint compared to the Rococo and grand furniture of the early and mid-18thC. The *escritoire* illustrated here is typical of French designs of the period. Several features also show the influence that French furniture had on English design at this time:

* brass inlay and gallery
* marbled top
* applied brass mouldings
* squared swan-neck handles
* neatly turned feet.

American furniture was even more strongly influenced by 19thC French styles than English furniture was – many American pieces were virtual copies of French designs, whereas in England some French design features were incorporated into basically traditional pieces.

The interior

The layout of the inside of this *escritoire* is typically French, especially in its use of a back mirror. The fitments are more vertical and more elaborate than in an English interior. Secret pull-out slides at the base of the central pillars are pleasingly discreet. The use of pale wood (for the interior drawers) is usually indicative of Continental cabinet-work, although maple, another pale wood, was used in England to a limited extent.

Locks

Continental locks are larger than English and American ones and are generally more finely made, usually requiring a double turn of the key to operate.

Continental   *English*   *English from c.1870*

Escutcheons

Continental escutcheons are squared at the bottom and more angular than early English ones, which are rounded off. Later English escutcheons are slightly smaller and squared off at the bottom. On English drawers the escutcheons tend to be near the top, whereas on Continental drawers they are lower down.

Drawers

The drawers are mahogany-(rather than oak-) lined, an invariable sign of quality. Because mahogany is less prone than oak to changing colour with age, mahogany linings tend to look deceptively new.

* The hole visible in the back of this drawer holds a peg which slots into a hole in the carcass to prevent the drawer from being pulled right out of the carcass. The pegs are often missing.

Construction

French Empire furniture, like its English counterparts of the period, is generally finely made. However, greater attention was paid on the Continent of Europe during this period to the finishing of pieces – for example the back of this *escritoire*, although not intended to be visible, is more tidily finished than it would be on an English piece.

WRITING (LIBRARY) TABLES

*An English George IV-period mahogany writing table
c.1825; ht 29in/73.5cm; wdth 48in/122cm; value range E.-F*

Identification checklist for early 19thC writing tables
1. Is the table mahogany (or rosewood)?
2. Are the legs relatively heavy, perhaps fluted or with
ring turning, and with correspondingly robust casters?
3. Is the top leathered? (Replacements are quite
acceptable.)
4. Do the drawers have original turned wooden knobs?
5. Are any locks of the Bramah type (introduced in the
late 18thC, see Locks)?
6. Is there thumbnail moulding around the edge of the
desk top?
7. Are the corners of the table generously rounded?
8. Do the drawers have fine dovetailing?

Writing tables
Although many writing tables
from the second half of the 18thC
have become almost prohibitively
expensive, those from the 19thC,
like that shown above, are more
affordable. The slender square
tapering or turned legs with
simple outline, of the 18thC, gave
way to the heavier type shown
here. During this period the
writing table with end supports
came to prominence (see facing
page). Another type usually
associated with the late 18thC is
the kidney-shaped writing table,
which is very sought-after. During
the Victorian period very large
writing tables, sometimes known
as "partners' desks", were made
for office use. Most are of
mediocre quality.
150

Typical features
The table *above* has several early
19thC characteristics:
* relatively wide crossbanding
* rounded corners to the top
* sturdy turned legs.

Sign of quality
The end of the table is nicely
finished off with a false front,
rather than being left plain.

Note
Three drawers are considered
more desirable than two.

Identification point
Thumbnail (convex) moulding is
a good aid to dating, as it is found
on many pieces from c.1825 and
later. (18thC edges were reeded or
plain.)

Writing tops
The leather on this table is modern – the original would never have survived in such fine condition. However, it is in the style of the original, with appropriate gilt tooling, and has the characteristic colour of antique leather.

Locks
The drawers of tables from this period may have Bramah locks, introduced in the late 18thC. These are set in a characteristic circular escutcheon and have patent cylindrical keys.

Watch point
Some writing tables from the early 19thC have had their original ring-turned legs cut off and replaced by slender square tapering legs to suggest the earlier, more expensive type of writing table. Examine the timber of the legs carefully to check that there is no discrepancy in colour between them and the table top.

Chippendale-period writing tables
The heyday of the writing table was the Chippendale period. Most of these are in mahogany. Drawers are commonly edged with cock-beading and the most popular type of handle was that of swan-neck form (see pp. 26-7). Drawer linings are in oak. Larger examples of fine quality will have drawers on both sides, or at least dummy drawers at the back (rather than being left plain). Legs are usually cabrioles, perhaps with carved decoration, or are square, sometimes with chamfered inner edges and moulded decoration or blind fret carving. Examples with their original leather tops are scarce. Chippendale-period writing tables are rare and most of those found today in the Chippendale style are Victorian or later reproductions. These can be identified by the poorer quality and colour of the timber and by their often ungainly proportions.

End-support writing tables
A popular style of Regency writing table is that with end supports. The example shown, *above*, has a veneered top, but others have leathered tops with banded edges. They were made from the last quarter of the 18thC until well into the 19thC, in a variety of sizes. They are generally scarcer than examples on legs. This example is typical in its:
* rosewood veneer
* robust mouldings
* turned stretcher
* platform base with decorative detailing
* tendency toward chunkiness, which becomes increasingly pronounced during the Victorian period
* carved scrolled feet – scrolls also appear in the angles at the top of the end supports. (On high-quality examples feet may be gilded or parcel-gilt, or even have applied gilt metal mounts.)

Drawers
Typically, the table shown left has one row of real drawers and one dummy row. A sign of authenticity is revealed on comparing the marks on the underside of the drawer, *above bottom*, with those on the inside of the carcass, *above top*; it is apparent that the drawer has not run on the base but on the runners at the side. The drawer is paler where it has rested on the carcass, and the carcass is lighter at the sides where the runners have moved across it.

Value
Still reasonably priced, end-support tables of this type are likely to become more expensive.

A mid-19thC English walnut davenport
c.1860; ht 36in/91.5cm; wdth 22in/56cm; value range D-F

Identification checklist for 19thC davenports

1. Are the legs, or uprights, made in the solid from a fine-quality wood, such as satinwood, rosewood, or burr walnut?

2. Is the rest of the piece veneered in burr walnut?

3. Are there two banks of drawers, one real and one dummy?

4. Are there additional features, such as hidden drawers or fitted stationery compartments released by spring locks?

5. Is the slope on a self-opening ratchet device rather than fixed?

6. Are supports shaped and carved?

7. Are the legs shaped rather than turned?

8. Does the piece have a "piano" top, as opposed to the hinged sloping tops of earlier davenports?

9. Is the back finished (davenports being freestanding)?

10. Do the drawers have their original turned wooden knobs (rather than brass handles)?

Value point

Quality varies considerably: a high-quality piece, provided that it is in good condition, will fetch double the price of one of lesser quality (and three times the price of one in need of restoration, even if it is of good quality).

Davenports

These compact writing tables, introduced in the late 18thC, were made in two principal styles. Until 1840 the plain Regency box-type prevailed; this has a slide top which pulls forward for ease of writing (see *bottom right*). From c.1840, the type with the piano-rise top, scrolled or turned supports and a recessed case, like that in the main picture, became most common. The rise, which runs on a leather belt and weights, is released by a sprung lock inside the desk, which opens to reveal small drawers and pigeon holes. Such a feature greatly enhances the value of the piece as long as it is in good working order – replacements and repairs to these mechanisms are becoming increasingly costly.

Signs of quality

This davenport has several features that enhance its desirability:
* The whole piece, which is veneered in tight burr walnut, is nicely finished, including the back, which is panelled.
* The superior finish to the interior: the reading slope, which operates on a ratchet mechanism, is adjustable. The fitments are nicely embellished with contrasting veneers in bird's eye maple. The davenport retains its original inkwells, pen trays and so on (partly obscured in the picture by the reading stand). Although the leather of the top is a replacement, this does not affect the value.

The drawers

The drawers have been beautifully made, with fine veneers and dovetails and well-finished mahogany linings.
* Veneers were machine-cut by c.1860 but were still relatively thick. Examine the front and back panels of veneered davenports carefully, as veneers used in large sections are prone to splitting.

Drawer knobs and escutcheons

Wooden knobs were favoured by the Victorians. The mother-of-pearl escutcheon plates are an invariable sign of quality. They also act as a good dating guide, as they were introduced c.1850.

The lock

The wood around the lock is undisturbed, suggesting that the lock is original. It is thus a good guide to dating as the lock plate bears the lockmaker's name and the stamp "VR Patent", for Queen Victoria, who came to the throne in 1837.

Casters

Another good aid to dating is the presence of the original Victorian casters with the characteristic brown ceramic wheels. (Off-white wheels were also used in the period.) However, many casters have been replaced and the absence of the original ones should not deter the potential buyer.

A Regency box-type davenport

PEDESTAL DESKS

An English William IV/early Victorian mahogany pedestal desk c.1835; ht 30¹/₂in/77.5cm; wdth 56in/142cm; value range D-E.

Identification checklist for 19thC pedestal desks
1. Is the desk mahogany or, less commonly, walnut?
2. Is it constructed in three sections – a top and two pedestals?
3. Is it veneered?
4. Are the handles original?
5. Are the drawers surrounded by heavy moulding?

Pedestal desks

Pedestal desks are found in relative quantity from the mid-18thC, although a few exist from the early 18thC. They enjoyed a long period of popularity and continued to be produced throughout the 19thC and into the Edwardian period. In the 18th and early 19thC they are most commonly found in mahogany and are usually veneered. They were made in a wider variety of woods in the later 19thC. Pedestal desks are usually constructed in three sections with three frieze drawers along the top and three graduated drawers to the pedestals. In the second half of the 19thC large quantities were made as office desks, and the quality of these varies considerably.

The example *above* is of very high quality, and is characterized by the comparatively heavy moulding around the drawers (as opposed to the cock beading generally found on 18thC desks). The moulding is repeated on the panelled outer and inner sides – an invariable sign of quality. Another good feature is the rounded corners of the top and pedestals. The knob handles, which are original, are of a type that was very popular during the 19thC. Many of the 18thC examples had brass handles. As with most pedestal desks, the leathered top of this desk is a replacement: original leather is very rare.

Value point

Walnut pedestal desks from the Victorian period are much sought after, as long as they are of good quality, and have recently risen enormously in price.

154

Size

Pedestal desks come in a wide range of sizes. The largest are known as "partners' desks"; these are fully fitted out on both sides, with the pedestals containing drawers on one side and cupboards on the other. The smallest pedestal desks are about 44in (112cm) across.

Maker's marks

The desk shown bears the maker's mark of Johnstone & Jeanes on the central top drawer – the place usually chosen by English cabinet-makers, although only the better makers marked their pieces. French cabinet-makers had a greater tendency to stamp their wares than English cabinet-makers. However, on both English and French pieces that are marked, the stamp or label may be that of the retailer rather than the maker.
* The drawers are lined in top-quality unpolished mahogany, and are exceptionally well made: they look pristine and are such a good fit that they are almost airtight. The locks, which are original, are stamped with the maker's name, a detail not found on 18thC locks.

Construction

In addition to the usual four blocks that locate the top on the base, this desk has an extra block, which allows the top to slide back and lock in place. This sign of attention to detail is indicative of quality generally.

"Improvements"

Pedestal desks are good candidates for improvement: some plain early desks have inlaid decoration added at a later date. This can be difficult for the untrained eye to spot, although the piece may simply look incongruous. If the desk is very fine, later decoration will devalue it, but if it is a fairly standard 19thC one the price may not be greatly affected, and may even be enhanced by such decoration. Another type of improvement is reveneering, or applying veneer to a carcass of indifferent quality.

How to identify modern veneer

Modern veneer can most easily be detected along an edge: being machine-cut it will be very thin and of even thickness. The edge may be covered up with moulding but if the piece has been later veneered, and has had its handles replaced, there will be evidence of the old handles on the inside of the drawer which will no longer be reflected on the outside (because the marks will have been covered by the new veneer). Similarly, if there is a split on the inside yet the veneer appears undamaged on the outside, this is a sure sign of reveneering.

TYPES OF MOULDING

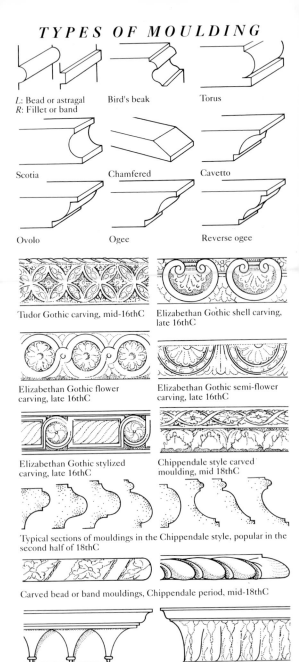

L: Bead or astragal
R: Fillet or band

Bird's beak

Torus

Scotia

Chamfered

Cavetto

Ovolo

Ogee

Reverse ogee

Tudor Gothic carving, mid-16thC

Elizabethan Gothic shell carving, late 16thC

Elizabethan Gothic flower carving, late 16thC

Elizabethan Gothic semi-flower carving, late 16thC

Elizabethan Gothic stylized carving, late 16thC

Chippendale style carved moulding, mid 18thC

Typical sections of mouldings in the Chippendale style, popular in the second half of 18thC

Carved bead or band mouldings, Chippendale period, mid-18thC

Typically delicate 18thC carved mouldings dating from c.1760 to the end of the century.

TYPES OF PEDIMENT

Swelled frieze, late 17thC

Double domed, end 17thC

Double arch, early 18thC

Triple arch, early 18thC

Broken arch, early Georgian

Cavetto flat top, early Georgian

Early swan's neck, mid-18thC

Broken architectural, with dentil and cornice, mid-18thC

Swan neck bonnet top, 2nd half 18thC.

Moulded dentil, late 18thC

Scrolled with carved finial, late 18thC

Rococo scrolled, mid-18thC

Sheraton domed late 18thC.

Early Victorian domed, c.1850

Mid-Victorian

Late Victorian carved

157

BOOKCASES AND DISPLAY CABINETS

Domestic bookcases and display cabinets were rare in the
17thC as only the wealthiest households possessed books or
ornaments; they came to prominence in the 18th and 19thC
when books were more widely available. Similarly, although
porcelain from China and Delftware from Holland were
imported to Europe during the 17thC, it was not until the
mid-18thC, when porcelain services and figurines began to
be produced in Europe, that there was a significant demand
for display cabinets.

Although a few cabinets have glazed sides and were
obviously intended for display purposes, there is little
difference between bookcases and display cabinets – either
can generally be used today for books, porcelain or both.

Queen Anne bookcases are very simple in form,
depending for decorative effect on finely figured walnut
veneers. The architectural style became popular a few years
later, in the 1740s, and favoured such details as broken
pediments, projecting brackets and urns. The bold
architectural form was also apparent in the glazed doors,
usually divided by plain bars into six panes.

The rococo style emerged around the middle of the
18thC. The architectural form became less pronounced, and
astragals replaced solid glazing bars. Provided they are
original, astragals provide a very useful guide to dating
(see p. 161).

By the mid-18thC most larger bookcases were "break-
fronted" (see pp. 160-1). The whole framework is lighter
and pediments are more delicate, the swan-neck form with
pierced decoration being particularly popular. Some
examples incorporate a pull-out secretaire drawer. The
breakfront style is illustrated in the 1762 edition of
Chippendale's *Director* (see pp. 64-5): they are invariably
mahogany, with ornate glazing bars; the finest have
delicately carved decoration. The very largest examples –
some are over 9 foot (27.5m) tall – are perhaps less practical
and have a limited market.

From c.1770 the influence of the Classical revival is seen
in bookcase design (as in other types of furniture), often
inspired by the designs of fashionable architects such as
Robert Adam. Leading cabinet-makers of this time, including
Thomas Sheraton, George Hepplewhite and the English firm
of Gillows, aimed for elegance, with vase finials and
delicate mouldings used in conjunction with highly figured
veneers either in mahogany or occasionally in the more
expensive West Indian satinwood, embellished with
bandings (often kingwood or tulipwood) and inlaid lines
and ovals. The graceful glazing bars also now embodied
oval and classical vase forms.

In the United States the bookcase did not feature strongly
until well into the American Chippendale period (1755-90).
American bookcases are usually mahogany and of a
convenient size and do not generally display the fine details

of those made in England – for example, the astragal formations are usually of straightforward geometric design. The serpentine form, which is peculiarly American, was very popular.

Many bookcases and cabinets made before c.1775 were intended for the libraries of substantial houses and are far too large for the average household. However, during the last quarter of the 18thC and throughout the Regency, attention was turned to designing smaller items such as chiffoniers (see pp. 164-5), dwarf open bookcases, revolving bookcases and other related items, such as library steps and book carriers. These functional pieces are much sought-after, especially if of high quality.

Bookcases and cabinets were made in large numbers during the Victorian period; some are of exceptionally high quality, especially those veneered in burr walnut. However, it is best to avoid the poorly-made breakfront bookcases of this period, which were principally intended for office use: while these are useful, they are of little merit and will never appreciate to the same degree as a finely made piece of original design.

The influence of French furniture from the Louis XV and XVI periods is particularly marked in the output of London firms of the mid-19thC, especially in the sinuous forms that were able to take advantage of developments in glass-making techniques that facilitated curving and sweeping panes. In general, only the top London firms attempted to produce credenzas and other Continental-style pieces, as these called for skills not available to the average firm of cabinet-makers. A few American cabinets of the Victorian period also show a Continental influence.

Edwardian-period bookcases were based on late 18thC styles and are usually of a scale suitable for modern households. Some are of very high quality and the best examples from this period are fetching prices as high as those for good late 18thC examples. In fact, a high-quality Edwardian bookcase is probably a better investment than an indifferent Georgian one.

It is worth bearing in mind that a number of large bookcases have been altered to make them a more saleable size – for example, the wings of a breakfront bookcase may have been removed to reduce its width. Although this will make it a more practical size, such an alteration will nevertheless reduce the value as the piece will be regarded as incomplete.

Another pitfall to be aware of is the modern practice of converting late 19thC wardrobes into bookcases by glazing the doors and possibly altering the wardrobe's dimensions. Again, while this may result in an attractive and useful piece of furniture, these conversions should be reflected in the price. Such conversions are quite easy to detect by an examination of the proportions alone, but in most cases there is no attempt to pass them off as originals.

BREAKFRONT BOOKCASES

An English Regency-period mahogany breakfront bookcase
c.1815; ht 101in/258cm, wdth 85in/217cm, max dpth 20in/51cm; value range A-B

Identification checklist for early 19thC breakfront bookcases

1. Is the bookcase mahogany?
2. Is it veneered?
3. Do the sections belong together (see Marriages below)?
4. Is the glazing original?
5. Is the design generally chunky compared with 18thC styles?

Breakfront bookcases
Breakfront, or library, bookcases were first seen in England c.1740. Until then large bookcases were rarely found in private homes. In the 18thC they were usually made in mahogany, although they exist in other woods, such as satinwood. The early examples were often made in the solid; from c.1775 many were veneered. They are made in several sections. Size varies considerably. The market for the larger ones is somewhat limited; they are therefore relatively inexpensive, although almost any genuine breakfront bookcase is an expensive item to buy today.
160

Marriages
As with any two- or three-part furniture, it is necessary to establish that the sections belong together by checking that the following features correspond on all parts:
* decorative details – for example, the shaped panels on the doors of this piece, the applied mouldings, and the paterae
* the colour and figuring of the wood
* escutcheons
* the astragal moulding between the doors top and bottom
* construction details, such as the method used to hang the doors
* back panels.

Recognition points
* The Neo-gothic style so popular in the second half of the 18thC continued into the 19thC but by c.1825, when this bookcase was made, had become heavier, with a certain architectural weight.
* The bold nulled moulding along the top of this bookcase is very much of the period.

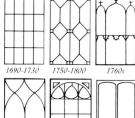

1690-1730   1750-1800   1760s

c.1780-1810   early 19thC   1830-80

Alterations
1. Reduction in height
The main carcass is sometimes reduced in height to make the piece more saleable. Bookcases usually have rungs at the side, as in the detail *above*, allowing the shelves to be positioned where required. However, the rungs invariably stop short of the top and bottom of the case and the first shelf. If a bookcase has been reduced in height the rungs may be too near the top or bottom for the shelf to hold a book of average size.

The height can also be reduced by removing the pediment or some of the cornice. If this has happened there will be marks on top of the bookcase where a pediment once sat.

The glazing bars may look ill-proportioned if they have been altered in the process of making a reduction in height.

2. Reduction in depth
This can be done by cutting through the sides and shelves and refixing the back. Such work may be detected by the obvious distressing of the newly cut surfaces. The piece may also appear shallower than is usual, although this may make it more saleable.

Glazing
The type used will depend on the period of the piece. Until the mid-18thC cabinets and bookcases were glazed with small rectangular panes, retained by fairly solid glazing bars, or astragals. The more intricate patterns current from the mid-18thC called for lighter glazing bars. Some bookcases from the 19thC were designed without astragals and just had plain glass set into a shaped panel.

It is preferable to have at least some of the original glazing. This can be detected by its rippled surface, sometimes more visible from the side than full on: the earlier the glass the more ripples it will have. Glass is secured to the glazing bars with putty, which, if original, should look quite dark and brittle. A pane secured with fresh-looking or artificially stained putty is almost certainly a replacement.

Astragals
Astragals are sometimes replaced to make a piece look earlier than it is, or to give it a more desirable appearance. If this has happened there may be spare, patched rebates where the original astragals were fixed into the framework.

Original astragals will be in the same wood as the rest of the piece, and will show natural signs of wear. Replacements may be stained to match the principal wood or to suggest age.

Construction
The top is simply screwed to the base. The screw holes in the bookcase should align with screw holes in the top of the base. Be wary of spare screw holes, and those that appear in one part only.

DISPLAY CABINETS

A late 18thC English Sheraton-period satinwood display cabinet c.1790; wdth 20in/51cm; value range B-E

Identification checklist for late 18thC display cabinets
1. Is the cabinet satinwood or mahogany?
2. Does it incorporate veneered panels in a different wood (probably rosewood or kingwood)?
3. Is it of restrained and elegant design?
4. Does it have square tapering legs?
5. Does it have inlaid stringing?
6. Do the top and bottom belong to each other?
7. Does the piece retain any original glazing (see p. 161)?

Display cabinets
Display cabinets were not made in England to any extent until the mid-18thC, when decorative objects such as porcelain figurines began to be made in Europe. Even then, they were not plentiful until the 19thC.

Typical Sheraton features

The distinctive, restrained style of the cabinet, *left*, is absolutely characteristic of the late 18thC (or an Edwardian reproduction in the Sheraton style, see *right*). Typical features include:
* square slender tapering legs
* use of satinwood as the main veneer
* simple design, with contrasting veneers and inlaid panels for decoration.

Woods

Chippendale-period display cabinets were mostly in mahogany with carved decoration. Later in the 18thC they were usually in figured mahogany with satinwood panels, or vice versa; or in satinwood with rosewood or kingwood panels.

Condition

Delicate furniture of this type should be examined for damage in the following areas:
* legs, which are long and slender. However, the galleried shelf here, a typical Sheraton feature, provides added strength
* stringing, which may have popped out and been replaced
* crossbanding, which can come away or loosen due to adverse atmospheric conditions
* escutcheons, which sometimes fall off and are replaced
* decorative brass galleries. Collectors should note that these are relatively minor problems some degree of damage or restoration is inevitable on a piece of this age.

Marriages

Some cabinets may have become separated from their original stands so it is important to check that the parts belong together. The piece on p. 162 is clearly not a marriage: the cabinet sits neatly within the moulding, and the decorative details match up on both parts. An additional check could be made to see whether any marks on the underside of the cabinet correspond with those on the top of the stand. As a final test, lift off the cabinet, which will be simply screwed to the base: the veneer should cover only that part of the top which is visible when the cabinet is in place. If the whole top is veneered the base may originally have been a different item, perhaps a side table.

Period or later?

The Victorians and Edwardians reproduced Sheraton cabinets in great numbers, but a reproduction will differ from an original in a number of ways:
* the satinwood of a reproduction will lack the warmth and depth of 18thC satinwood
* the veneers will be thin and even compared to those of the 18thC (see p.10)
* the style of keyhole escutcheon (see p. 14), although a period piece may be fitted with a later replacement
* the type of lock (see p. 153)
* the back of a reproduction will be finished to a greater extent than on an 18thC item
* the interior of a reproduction will be lightly polished – Georgian interiors are generally unpolished.

Edwardian display cabinet

This late 19thC/Edwardian display cabinet is very much in the Sheraton style – typified by the use of satinwood, the style of glazing (see p. 161), the oval painted panels, and the slender square tapering legs. However, the satinwood is rather pale and the painted decoration, which is more colourful than was usual in the Georgian period, is somewhat sentimental.

CHIFFONIERS

An English Regency mahogany chiffonier in the Neo-classical taste c.1810; ht 50in/127cm; wdth 30¹/₂in/77.5cm; value range C-E.

Identification checklist for chiffoniers
1. Is the chiffonier veneered, either in rosewood or mahogany?
2. Does it have lyre-shaped supports with brass rods?
3. Are there sphinx heads at the top of the door pilasters?
4. Does the piece have a pierced gallery?
5. Does it have pleated silk door panels?

Chiffoniers
The chiffonier, which became popular during the late 18thC, is basically a small shallow cabinet with a shelf, or even two or three shelves, above, and sometimes with a drawer below the top of the cabinet section. The back of the superstructure is sometimes mirrored. On better examples the top section is ornate – for example, it may have "S" or lyre-shaped supports, sides filled in with lattice work, or other decorative features in brass or metal. The cabinet sections may have applied sphinx heads in brass, as in the example above, or other cast and gilded mounts, and brass grille doors. Chiffoniers are very popular today, especially
164

those fitted with a drawer, which makes them eminently suitable for use as a sideboard in a small town house. Size varies considerably, as does quality – some are very plain, others can be quite sophisticated. The chiffonier shown *above* is of high quality: the best mahogany veneers have been employed, complemented by attractive ebony line inlay (a Regency characteristic). Among its other quality features are:
* gilded and ebonized sphinx heads and feet
* lyre-shaped supports
* brass gallery
* tapering features
* Egyptian motifs in the decoration.

Marks and other signs of wear

Look for signs of wear on the moving parts – for example, on any drawers. Marks are visible, *above*, on the base of the piece, caused by the action of opening and closing the door – a reassuring sign of authenticity. Others signs of age and wear may include:
* worn gilding
* a build-up of polish and dirt in the crevices of any carving.

Lyre-shaped supports

The lyre-shaped support was a popular feature on English, American, Empire and Biedermier furniture of the period, especially for table supports.

Brass galleries

The brass gallery is a feature found on much sophisticated furniture of the period. This one is original: the casting is of high quality, with a small build-up of polish in the crevices, and the wood around it looks undisturbed.

Silk-pleated doors

This Regency-period rosewood and brass-inlaid chiffonier shows the alternative style of door, with the silk pleating sitting behind brass grilles, which today are seldom original. In the past, the blind panelled doors of some less sophisticated early 19thC chiffoniers were replaced by silk and brass grilles to give a more sophisticated and refined look and to enhance the potential value. Such conversions are not easy to detect but a converted piece may look heavier in form and may lack some of the sophisticated Regency features described on the previous page.

Quality feature

The front of the shelf is ebonized – a sign of attention to detail. Another unusual feature is the adjustable shelf – extra peg holes are visible on the support and at the back.

Reproductions

Chiffoniers were mass-produced in the Victorian period. Many of these were cheaply made and are quite without merit, lacking the refinement of those made in the Regency.

A Swedish Biedermeier bookcase
c.1830; ht 90in/228.5cm; width 43in/109cm; value range C-D

Identification checklist for Biedermeier bookcases
1. Is the form essentially traditional?
2. If the piece is glazed, are the glazing bars plain and straight?
3. Are any escutcheons shield- or lozenge-shaped?
4. Is the wood pale – for example, birch, perhaps with black decorative details?
5. Do the top and bottom belong together?
6. Is any of the glazing original?

Biedermeier bookcases

Before the 1830s most Biedermeier bookcases were of architectural form. The 1830s saw a return to more traditional styles, exemplified by the birchwood example on the previous page. Many Biedermeier bookcases and display cabinets are open, without glazed doors (see *right*).

Earlier bookcases

Small open bookcases became popular during the late 18th and early 19thC in England, Continental Europe and the United States, largely due to the increased number of smaller townhouses. They are always keenly sought-after, especially those of good quality, being useful both as bookcases and for the display of decorative objects. Many of those made in Continental Europe were in pale woods, which were less popular in England, where mahogany and rosewood were more common, although maple was used occasionally.

Authenticity

As with all two- and three-part furniture, it is important to ascertain that the components belong with each other (see p.31). The cabinet and base of this bookcase were obviously made at the same time from the same wood: the colour match at the sides, top and bottom is perfect, the veneers line up precisely, and the top sits neatly within the recessed moulding of the base.

Sign of quality

Unusually for bookcases (and display cabinets), the insides of the sides are veneered – a sign of quality. The shelves are fixed; adjustable shelves are more usual.

Later bookcases

This German parcel-gilt open mahogany bookcase, *above*, originally one of a pair, is in the Empire style that was popular throughout France, Germany, Russia and Scandinavia, and which caught on with New York cabinet-makers, although it was not nearly as popular in Regency England. The severe lines, gilt mouldings and capitals and the lion's-paw feet are characteristic.
* The mahogany is veneered onto a pine carcass but not finished off inside, presumably for economy.
* Open bookcases made in New York in the Empire style tend to be very ornate.

CREDENZAS

A Victorian walnut credenza, or side cabinet
c.1860; ht 43¹/₂in/110.5cm; wdth 59in/150cm; value range D-F

Identification checklist for Victorian credenzas
1. Is the credenza in burr walnut veneer?
2. Does it show a French or Italian influence?
3. Are the veneers machine-cut (see p. 10)?
4. Is the standard of cabinet-making high?
5. Are any gilt metal mounts crisp (well-cast)?
6. Does the top have bowed ends?
7. Is at least some of the glass original?

Credenzas
This type of side cabinet was made in large quantities throughout the second half of the 19thC. The example shown *above* is of good quality, but not the finest: some credenzas display very high standards of cabinet-making – for example, the best pieces have superb marquetry and inlaid decoration with beautifully cast applied gilt mounts; the worst are cheaply made and consequently have not survived

well. Ebonized examples tend to be less sought after than walnut veneered ones.

Most interiors were, at least initially, lined in velvet; red was the most popular colour. Where the original velvet has survived, it is likely to be very faded.

The buying guideline is quality rather than size. However, some credenzas will not be very saleable if they are too big for the average house, especially if they are not of high quality.

Condition

The overall condition of the credenza is good, although the top of the central oval panel is missing: a faint outline of it is visible on the wood – a minor and acceptable flaw that should not cause the piece to suffer a loss in value.

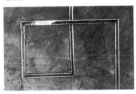

Inlay

As is to be expected, the inlaid lines have deteriorated in places and some pieces are missing. This is not a serious fault and is easily restored.

Locks

The locks are the original Victorian ones – there are no signs of replacements or disturbed wood – and are stamped with the word "patent", which was not used after 1901.
* The best 19thC credenzas may have the maker's stamp impressed into the top of a door.

Glass

The credenza retains its original glass panels. These are identifiable as such by their slightly rippled surface and the presence of air bubbles. Old glass tends to be thinner than modern replacements. Be wary of broken or cracked glass to curved end panels: replacement glass, if curved, is costly, as it has to be made in a mould.

Signs of quality

This credenza has a number of features that enhance its desirability:
* shaped glass panels at the display ends
* decorative details, such as the Sèvres-style porcelain panel
* attractive veneers
* good amount of attractive inlay
* high-quality gilt metal mounts and castings
* panelled rather than plain back
* glazed end cupboards rather than open shelves
* inlaid shelves in the side panels.

Continental influence

Although English, this credenza, like many others of the period, is very much influenced by Continental designs – particularly evident here in the Sèvres-style panels and mounts. Such decorative features should be scrutinized, as quality varies considerably

MISCELLANEOUS

MIRRORS

An English Regency gilt girandole mirror
c.1800/10; ht 52in/132cm; value range B-D

Identification checklist for Regency convex mirrors
1. Is the mirror carved?
2. Does it have gilded or painted decoration and is this original, or if not, has it been sensitively restored?
3. Are the motifs typical of the period (see p.40)?
4. Is the plate original and/or in acceptable condition?
5. Do any candle arms have cut glass sconces and drops?

Convex mirrors

Convex mirrors were first seen in England in the early years of the Regency, the process of producing the convex plate having been brought over from France. They come in a wide variety of sizes and degrees of grandeur: the most basic type, which can still be purchased for a modest sum, is of a simple circular form, usually gilt, with ball decoration. As high-fashion items, convex mirrors were made for a brief period only. They were very popular in the United States, where they are often surmounted by eagles.
* However beautifully presented the mirror is at the front, the back will be quite rough in appearance – the wood perhaps just finished in a yellow ochre colour.

Regilding

Mirrors deteriorate because of the effects of age and damp. Good restoration, such as that carried out on the mirror shown on the previous page, is acceptable: original gilding on a piece of this age is likely to be in a poor state. Good regilding, using water gilding rather than oil, should show contrasts of burnished and matt areas. Oil gilding will look comparatively lifeless and be of a uniform colour, as it cannot be burnished. Inexpert gilding may be too heavily gessoed and the gilded areas will lacking fine detail.

* Oil gilding is appropriate in some contexts (see p. 75).

Beware

Although good regilding is acceptable, the carved decoration beneath the gilding should be original. While an ornate mirror with plenty of carving will almost certainly have had some necessary replacement carving, avoid those that have been excessively reworked. Replaced sections can be difficult to detect once they are covered by gilding, but it may be possible to identify differences in the style of carving where reworking has occurred. The vulnerable features, such as cresting, are the most likely areas to have been replaced. Look at the back as, not being gilded, it may reveal more.

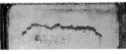

Glass

It is preferable to have the original plate. This glass (from another mirror) shows some deterioration, but not enough to warrant replacement.

* Old plate is greyer than modern glass, and usually gives a softer reflection. It is of uneven thickness.

Compo

Many inexpensively made 19thC mirrors and later reproductions are made of wirework covered with a moulded composition, or "compo", a putty-like substance which, when gilded, bears a superficial resemblance to carved wood. However, it has a tendency to shrink and crack, disturbing the gilded surface.

Early 18thC mirrors

This typical walnut and parcel-gilt mirror of c.1720 is of the architectural style that was popular during the 1720s and 30s. It is centred by a female mask and Prince of Wales feathers. An important aspect of these mirrors is the quality and colour of the walnut veneers used.

George III giltwood mirror

Made from the mid-18thC right through the second half of the 19thC, carved and giltwood mirrors were very popular. They were made in a variety of sizes and design, with either oval or rectangular plates. Many have "C" scrolls, scrolling foliage or Oriental motifs.

171

BEDS

A late 18thC English 4-post bed frame
c.1775; ht 80in/203cm; value range C-E.

Identification checklist for late 18thC 4-poster beds
1. Are the posts mahogany, and slender, or painted beech?
2. Is the cornice mahogany or painted, and possibly carved?
3. Are the stretchers original?
4. Is there carved decoration to the posts?
5. Are the head-posts quite plain?
6. Is the bed its original dimensions (see facing page)?

Bed posts

In the 16th and 17thC oak tester (four-poster) beds had chunky oak posts which were usually turned or carved. From the 18thC the posts at the foot end are usually in polished mahogany, and are always of slender and elegant proportions, exemplified by the bed shown, *above*. Styles of post vary: this bed has cluster columns – a feature found on much furniture of the period.
* Back posts are made in beech and, like the shaped headboard, are simply finished (as they were not intended to be seen) and are hidden by the drapes.

Styles of bed post

early   c.1740   c.1750   c.1780   c.1805   mid-   American,
17thC   /60   /90   /10   19thC   1800-20

Construction
The bed is held together with bolts that go through the posts into the bearers; brass swing-covers conceal the bolt holes.

Mattresses
The grooves at regular intervals along the inner surface of the side rails (see detail, *above*) were made to accommodate the slats onto which the mattress was placed. Today, a slender bed base is usually used instead. This sits on top of the rail, with a mattress over it.
* Bed bases usually have to be made to fit the bed as beds were not made in standard sizes, and because they sometimes have to be shaped to fit around the posts.
* Measure the bed to check that it is big enough: although the overall structure tends to seem quite large, the mattress area may be rather small; a typical size was 4 x 6 feet (1.2 x 1.8m) – somewhat small for many people today.
* The bearers are beech and left unpolished and, like the back posts, they were not seen once the bed was dressed.

Cornices
The cornice of the bed shown on the previous page is constructed in pine and embellished with carved and painted decoration. A mahogany bed might have a mahogany cornice, moulded and perhaps carved, but it is also quite common to find a combination of mahogany posts and painted cornices.
* Cornices vary quite considerably, from simple bars to which the drapery is attached, to those with a flat top and a small amount of decoration, to the type with an elaborately shaped top, and carved and pierced decoration.

Headboards
The headboards of most 18thC beds were made in a secondary wood as they were obscured by the drapes. On later beds, and on some American examples, they are often in polished mahogany. Replaced headboards are acceptable and should not have a significant effect on the value.

Alterations
With changing styles of mattresses and beds, many 4-poster beds have been altered over the years – for example, they may have been reduced in height or width. If the bed has been reduced in height there will be plugged holes low down on the posts where the rails have been moved up or down from their original position. If the bed has been reduced in width, new rails will have to be made in order to restore the bed to its original dimensions. The bed shown on the previous page is unusual in not having been altered in size.

Made-up oak tester beds
Period oak tester beds in original condition are rare today, partly because when they became unfashionable in the 18th and 19thC many were dismantled and discarded. Thus most of the oak tester beds on the market are made up of old parts, as this one, *above*, is: it has a combination of 16th, 17th and 18thC elements, with some possibly Victorian additions. The posts may have been lengthened to accommodate the carved arched panels with inlaid decoration which probably do not belong with the lower panelled section. The carving at the top of the tester suggests that this part is Victorian (see p. 14).

DUMB WAITERS

An English George II mahogany dumb waiter
c.1750; ht 45in/115cm; value range C-F

Identification checklist for mid-late 18thC dumb waiters
1. Is the piece mahogany?
2. Does it have a tripod base with cabriole legs?
3. Is it of elegant and pleasing proportions?
4. Does it have claw-and-ball or pad feet?
5. Does it have at least two graduated, possibly revolving, circular tiers?

Dumb waiters
Dumb waiters, stands with two or more tiers of trays around a central column, were made in England in the second half of the 18thC, although a few Regency examples exist. Most are mahogany.

High-quality features
This is a top quality example with

several fine features:
* spindled gallery around each tier
* fine carving on the cabrioles
* carved claw-and-ball feet
* spiral carving on the stem.
Plainer examples are likely to have a slightly dished rim, turned balusters without the carving, and a plain pad foot.

WHATNOTS

An English Victorian ebonized calemander whatnot
c.1860; ht 37in/94cm; value range D-F

Identification checklist for Victorian whatnots
1. Is the piece in walnut or calamander, veneered onto a mahogany ground?
2. Does it have applied gilt metal bead mouldings?
3. Does it have ceramic casters?
4. Are there at least three tiers?
5. Does it show a French influence?

Whatnots
Whatnots, stands with open shelves, were first seen during the late 18thC, when most were made in the solid in mahogany. They usually have three, four or five tiers. Some have one or two drawers at the bottom. This example is mahogany veneered in calamander onto mahogany – a wood that is characterized by its contrasting pale and almost black streaks. Earlier whatnots look very English but this piece has a definite French influence in its:
* beadwork
* use of contrasting ebony and wood
* gilt metal anklets at the bottom of turned legs
* smaller proportions.

Value point
Although this whatnot is relatively late in date, it will fetch more than many earlier plain mahogany examples, as it is sophisticated, attractive and in good condition.

CANTERBURIES

An early 19thC English mahogany canterbury
c.1800/10; max ht 20in/52cm; wdth 18in/48cm; value range E-F

Identification checklist for early 19thC canterburies
1. Is the canterbury mahogany or rosewood?
2. Is the design relatively restrained?
3. Is the piece fitted with a drawer?
4. Does it stand on slender, turned legs? (Square tapering legs are rarer, and traditionally have been considered more desirable.)
5. Does it have a concave-shaped top?
6. Does it have brass casters?
7. Does it have corner finials?

Canterburies
Canterburies, originally designed for storing sheet music, first appeared in England in the late 18thC/early 19thC and were predominantly in mahogany and rosewood. From the 1820s they are found in other timbers, such as bird's eye maple from c.1825, and walnut during the Victorian period, when designs became more ornate.

Condition
Canterburies are relatively delicate, particularly around the legs, which are often damaged or replaced. Repairs can be better detected by turning the piece upside down. Uprights should be examined for splits or breaks. Replacement finials (on top of the corner uprights) should be reflected in the price.

What to look for
Many canterburies, especially those from the early 19thC, are very similar in basic design and the following points will always help the re-sale value of a canterbury: a generally good colour and patina, original condition, elegant design, fine-quality construction and a fitted drawer (or drawers). The value of the example *above* is enhanced by the following features:
* nicely curved concave top rails; the central one incorporates a carrying handle
* original turned wooden knob handles on the drawer
* tall elegant legs.

Fakes
Fakes have not appeared, but there are obvious modern reproductions on the market.

QUARTETTO TABLES

A nest of four English Regency mahogany quartetto tables
c.1800; ht 29in/73.5cm; value range D-F

Identification checklist for early 19thC quartetto tables
1. Are the tables mahogany or rosewood?
2. Does each one have a low-galleried rectangular top?
3. Are the tables of slender construction?
4. Do they have cross-banded decoration to the tops, together with inlaid stringing?
5. Does the set comprise three or four tables?
6. Are the tables of graduated size so that they slot away when not in use?
7. Are the supports slender and simply turned?
8. Does the top of the largest table show more signs of exposure to light than the others?
9. Is the largest table approx. 29-30in (73.5-76cm) high?

Quartetto tables
These essentially English pieces were introduced during the late 18thC and continued to be made throughout the 19thC. They are invariably of rectangular form and simple elegant design. The early examples were principally in mahogany and rosewood. Victorian examples are mostly in walnut; there are also some highly ornate papier mâché tables. The Edwardians reverted to late 18thC styles, although their versions are approximately one third shorter.

Authenticity
The table tops should show signs of where the tables have been slotted together and pulled apart over the years. This should be particularly evident from the underside of all the tables (except the smallest). The largest table will invariably be more faded than the others as it will have had more exposure to light.

Condition
Look for breaks in the legs, which are usually rather fine and therefore prone to being damaged. The tops are thin and prone to splitting. Stretchers are frequently broken and many have either been re-made or are in need of repair. All these factors will have a bearing on the price.

TRAYS

An English Regency papier mâché tray
c.1810; lgth 29in/73.5cm; value range E-F

Identification checklist for early 19thC papier mâché trays
1. Is the tray japanned in black or, more rarely, in scarlet, green or blue?
2. Is the decoration predominantly gilt?
3. Does the decoration include chinoiserie floral sprays and butterflies?
4. Is the tray rectangular, with rounded corners and angled upright sides?

Note
Some, but not all, papier mâché trays have an impressed maker's stamp on the back.

Trays
Trays made before c.1750 are rare. Chippendale-period trays are mostly mahogany and those found today are usually oval in shape with brass banding. Later 18thC examples tend to be veneered, the finest in satinwood and perhaps with marquetry work, a gallery and cast brass handles. Some early 19thC trays have a spindled gallery. Victorian trays are ornately decorated.

Papier mâché
Papier mâché came to prominence in the early 19thC. By the Victorian period a whole variety of objects and furniture were produced in this medium, and trays in particular were very popular. Regency examples are the most sought-after, especially if they have chinoiserie decoration. The tray *above* has the typical
178

Regency shape; those from the Victorian period are more ornate.

Value points
* Black is the most common ground colour for papier mâché trays; other colours are particularly sought-after.
* Larger examples tend to fetch more money than smaller ones because they are more suitable for conversion to coffee tables – a practice particularly popular in the United States.

Condition
Papier mâché is vulnerable to damage, especially at the sides, which frequently come away from the base. The decoration is often in a poor state. Restoration can be undertaken but overpainting will then be necessary. Extensive restoration will considerably reduce the value, as will warping.

Chippendale-period trays

Chippendale-period trays are usually mahogany, made in the solid and, like the one *above*, brass-banded in the manner of wine coolers (see pp. 138-9), so it is important to check that the bands are original. The colour of the timber, and the patina will also be key factors in assessing the value of such pieces.

Copies

Later 18thC trays were copied by the Edwardians in large numbers – the wooden galleries of Edwardian examples are generally much thinner and more fragile than those of Georgian examples, which were made up from laminated wood for strength.

Victorian trays

This early Victorian black and gilt japanned papier mâché tea tray is a high-quality tray typical in shape and subject matter of those made during the Victorian period, when famous paintings popular at the time were often copied onto trays. Other commonly depicted subjects included church interiors, famous houses and castles and floral sprays in the European style. There was also a series known as the Queen's "favourites". Papier mâché had ceased to be popular by the Edwardian period.
* Victorian trays incorporating mother-of-pearl inlay (often around the border), seen after c.1825, are not popular today and are therefore relatively inexpensive.

Maker's marks

Many prominent makers – for example, Henry Clay, the best-known maker of early papier mâché trays, whose work is invariably of high quality; Jennens & Bettridge, the most important makers of papier mâché furniture; and Walton & Co – marked their wares with an impressed mark, which was often relatively detailed. The red Regency tray is impressed on the underside "CLAY, KING ST/COVT. GARDEN", and the example shown *above* is stamped "B WALTON & CO WARRANTED" and is also inscribed "The Happy Meeting Painted by George Morland."
* The presence of a maker's mark is reassuring. However, the many unmarked trays that are beautiful and of fine quality should not necessarily be regarded as less desirable.

GLOSSARY

Acanthus A leaf motif used in carved and inlaid decoration.
Apron The shaped skirt of wood that runs beneath the legs of a table or feet of a chest.
Armoire The Continental term for a large tall cupboard originally used for storing armour.
Astragal A small semi-circular moulding in architecture and in furniture a term often applied to the glazing bars of cabinets and bookcases. Astragals are sometimes in brass.
Backboard The unpolished back of wall furniture.
Balloon-back chair A chair with a rounded back, the best-known type of Victorian dining or salon chair.
Baluster The shaped **turning**, or slender pillar with a bulbous base, used on the legs and pedestals of tables.
Banding Decorative veneer used around the edges of tables and drawers. See p. 14.
Barley twist The spiral shape much favoured for **turned** legs of the second half of the 17thC.
Bergère The term for a French armchair, applied in England to chairs with caned backs and sides.
Bevel The decorative angled edge of a mirror.
Bird-cage support The mechanism, located at the top of the pedestal, that enables some 18thC **tripod tables** to swivel.
Blind fret carving A solid background with **fretwork** carving in front.
Bobbin A type of **turning** found on the legs of 17thC furniture.
Bombé The double-curved or swollen shape found in **commodes** and **bureaux** in Continental · Europe and occasionally in 18thC English furniture.
Bonheur-du-jour A small ladies' writing table of the late 18thC.
Boulle or buhl work A form of marquetry work using brass and tortoiseshell, developed in the 18thC.
Bow front The outward curved front found on chests of drawers from the late 18thC.
Bracket foot A squared foot, the most commonly found foot on 18thC cabinet furniture.
Breakfront The term for a piece of furniture with a protruding central section.
Broken pediment A symmetric break in the centre of a **pediment**, often infilled with an urn or eagle motif.

Brushing slide The pull-out slide found above the top drawer of some small 18thC chests.
Bun foot A flattened version of the ball foot, often found on **case furniture** of the second half of the 17thC.
Bureau A writing desk with a **fall front** that encloses a fitted interior, with drawers below.
Bureau bookcase A bureau with a bookcase above.
Burr (or burl in the USA) The tightly knotted grain from the base of a tree, used to decorative effect in **veneers**.
Cabriole leg A gently curving S-shaped leg found on tables and chairs of the late 17th and 18thC.
Canted corner A decorative angled corner, found on case furniture of the 18thC.
Canterbury A container for sheet music, from the 19thC.
Carcass The main body of a piece of furniture.
"Carved up" A term describing furniture that has been carved at a date later than construction, usually in the Victorian period.
Carver or elbow chair A dining or salon chair with open arms.
Case furniture Items intended primarily as receptacles – for example, chests of drawers.
Casters Small pivoted wheels, usually in brass, attached to the ends of some legs or feet.
Cellaret 18thC term for wine coolers and containers, and for the drawer in some sideboards designed for storing wine.
Chaise longue An elongated 18thC upholstered chair or daybed, popular in England during the Regency period.
Chamfer An angled corner.
Chesterfield A late 19thC deep-buttoned upholstered settee with no wood showing.
Chest on stand A two-part tall chest of drawers, popularly known as a tallboy or highboy.
Cheval mirror A tall dressing mirror supported by two uprights.
Chiffonier A side cabinet with or without a drawer and with one or more shelves above.
Chinoiserie Oriental-style decoration, on lacquered or painted furniture.
Claw-and-ball foot A foot modelled as a ball gripped by a claw, used with a cabriole leg.
Cleated ends On long tables, the end sections applied to narrow boards with the grain running in the opposite direction to prevent

warping.

Cockbeading A bead moulding applied to the edges of drawers.

Coffer A joined and panelled low chest, usually of oak, with a lid.

Commode A highly decorated chest of drawers or cabinet, often of bombé shape, with applied mounts.

Composition or compo A putty-like material that can be moulded, applied to mirrors and fire surrounds and gilded or painted.

Console or pier table A table intended to stand against a wall, between windows. It usually has a matching mirror above it.

Corner chair A chair with back **splats** on two sides and a bowed top rail, intended for the corner of a room.

Cornice The projecting moulding at the top of tall furniture.

Coromandel Type of wood from the Coromandel coast of India used for banding and inlay, popular during the Regency.

Counter-well or guinea-well The small **dished** oval found in early Georgian card tables.

Country/provincial furniture The functional furniture made away from the major cities and main centres of production.

Credence table Late 17thC oak or walnut half-round table with a folding top.

Credenza A long side cabinet with glazed or blind (solid) doors, associated with the Victorian period.

Crinoline stretcher A crescent-shaped **stretcher** that unites the legs of some **Windsor chairs.**

Cross banding A veneered edge to table tops and drawer fronts, at right angles to the main **veneer.**

Cup and cover A bulbous **turning** with a differentiated top, common on legs until the late 17thC.

Davenport A compact writing desk with a sloped top above a case of drawers.

Dentils Small rectangular blocks applied at regular intervals to the cornices of much 18thC furniture.

Dished table top A hollowed-out solid top, associated with tripod tables with **pie-crust** edges.

Distressed A term for a piece that has been artificially aged.

Dovetails A series of interlocking joints, used in drawers.

Dowel See **Pegged furniture.**

Drop-in seat An upholstered seat frame that sits in the main framework of a chair.

Drop handle Pear-shaped handle popular during the late 17thC/early 18thC.

Drop-leaf Any table with a fixed central section and hinged flaps.

Drum table A circular writing table supported by a central pedestal with frieze drawers.

Dummy drawer A decorative false drawer, complete with handle.

Ebonized Wood stained and polished black to simulate ebony.

End support A central support at the sides of a writing or sofa table.

Escritoire A cabinet with a hinged front, which provides a writing surface, and a fitted interior.

Escutcheon Brass plate surrounding and protecting the edges of a keyhole – sometimes with a cap or cover on a pivot.

Fall front The flap of a **bureau** or **secretaire** that pulls forward to provide a writing surface.

Fauteuil An upholstered armchair.

Feather or herringbone banding Two narrow bands of veneer laid in opposite diagonals.

Fielded panel A raised panel with a bevelled or chamfered edge that fits into a framework.

Figuring The natural grain of wood seen in **veneers.**

Finial A decorative **turned** knob applied to the top of fine bureau bookcases and the like.

Flamed veneer A **veneer** cut at an angle to enhance the figuring.

Fluting Decorative concave, parallel grooves running down the legs of tables and chairs.

Foliate carving Carved flower and leaf motifs.

Fretwork Fine pierced decoration.

Frieze The framework immediately below a table top.

Gadroon A decorative border, carved or moulded, comprising a series of short flutes or reeds.

Gainsborough chair A deep armchair with an upholstered seat and back, padded open arms and, usually, carved decoration.

Galleried table A table with a wood or metal border around the top edge.

Gateleg A leg that pivots to support a **drop leaf** on a table.

Gesso A plaster-like substance applied to carved furniture before gilding; also used as a substitute for carving when moulded and applied.

Gilt-tooled decoration Impressed gold leaf on the edges

of leather desk tops.

Girandole A candle holder or sconce with a mirrored back, designed to hang on a wall.

Greek key A **fretwork** design based on ancient Greek decoration.

Hairy-paw foot A paw foot, carved to give a furred appearance, first seen in the 18thC.

Harlequin A term used to describe a set of chairs that are similar but do not match.

Herringbone banding See **Feather banding**

Highboy The American term for a chest on a stand, usually with **cabriole** legs.

Husk A decorative motif of formalized leaves.

Improved An item that has been altered or added to at a later date to improve its value.

Inlay Brass, mother-of-pearl or veneer set into the surface of solid or veneered furniture for decorative effect.

Intaglio An incised design, as opposed to a design in relief.

Japanned An item painted and varnished in imitation of Oriental lacquer work, popular in the early 18thC.

Joined Method of furniture construction using mortice and tenon joints secured by pegs or dowels and without glue. Became widespread in the 15thC until the end of the 17thC.

Joined stool A stool, usually in oak, of joined construction.

Kneehole desk A desk with a recessed central cupboard below the frieze drawer.

Lacquer A gum-like substance, coloured and used as a ground for chinoiserie and gilding.

Ladder-back A chair with a series of horizontal back-rails.

Lappet A carved flap at the top of a leg with a pad foot.

Lion's paw foot A foot carved as a lion's paw, popular in the 18thC and the Regency period; also found as brass casters during the early 19thC.

Loo table A large Victorian card or games table, usually circular.

Loper A pull-out arm used to support the hinged fall of a bureau.

Lowboy A small side table on cabriole legs, from the first half of the 18thC.

Marquetry A highly decorative form of **inlay** using veneers.

Married The term used for an item that has been made up from

two or more pieces of furniture, usually of the same period.

Mortice See **Pegged furniture.**

Moulding A shaped piece of wood applied to a piece of furniture, comprising a long strip or a small decorative motif.

Mule chest A **coffer** with a single row of drawers in the base.

Nest of tables A set of three or four occasional tables that slot into each other when not in use.

Ogee A double curve of slender S-shape.

Ormolu A mount or article that is gilded or gold-coloured.

Overmantel mirror A mirror designed to hang over a mantlepiece.

Ovolo A moulding comprising a quarter-segment of a sphere.

Oyster veneer A veneer formed by cutting branches of trees, such as laburnum, at right angles to the grain, producing small circles.

Pad or club foot A rounded foot that sits on a circular base, used in conjunction with cabriole legs.

Papier mâché Pulped paper that is moulded or lacquered to make trays and small pieces of furniture.

Parcel gilding Partial gilding.

Parquetry A geometrical pattern made up of small pieces of veneer, sometimes of different woods.

Patera A small circular ornament made of wood, metal or composition.

Patina The build-up of wax and dirt that gives old furniture a soft mellow look.

Pedestal desk A flat desk, usually with a leathered top, that stands on two banks of drawers.

Pediment The gabled structure that surmounts a cornice.

Pegged furniture Early joined furniture constructed by a system of mortices (slots) and tenons (tongues), held together by dowels (pegs).

Pembroke table A small two-flap table that stands on four legs or a pedestal.

Pie-crust top The carved decorative edge of a dished-top **tripod table.**

Pier glass A tall, narrow mirror intended to hang against a pillar between the windows of a drawing room.

Pietra dura A composition of semi-precious stones applied to the panels of furniture.

Platform base Three- or four-cornered flat bases of tables supporting a central pedestal above and standing on scrolled or paw feet.

Plinth base A solid base, not raised on feet.

Pole-screen An adjustable fire screen.

Potboard The bottom shelf of a dresser or court cupboard, often just above the floor.

Provincial furniture See **Country furniture.**

Quartered top. A flat surface covered with four pieces of matched **veneer.**

Quartetto tables A nest of four tables.

Reeding Parallel strips of convex flutes found on the legs of chairs and tables.

Re-entrant corner A shaped indentation at each corner of a table.

Rule joint A type of hinge contrived in such a way that, when open, no separation shows between the two joined parts – a sign of quality in 18thC furniture.

Runners The strips of wood on which drawers slide.

Sabre leg A curved chair leg in the shape of a sabre, strongly associated with the Regency period.

Scagliola A composite material that resembles marble.

Scalloped or butterfly-wing leaf The serpentine flap of some pembroke tables.

Sconce A cup-shaped candle holder.

Seat rail The horizontal framework immediately below the chair seat that unites the tops of chair legs.

Secretaire A writing cabinet with a mock drawer front that lets down to provide a writing surface, revealing recessed pigeon holes.

Secretaire bookcase A secretaire with a bookcase fitted above.

Serpentine Undulating front for a **case** piece – convex in the centre and concave at the ends. Used for cabinets, chests, sideboards and so on, in the second half of the 18thC.

Settle The earliest form of chair to seat two or more people.

Shoe piece Projecting piece rising from the back rail of a chair seat into which the base of the **splat** is fixed.

Side chair A chair without arms, designed to stand against a wall.

Side table Any table designed to stand against a wall.

Silhouette leg A two-dimensional leg shaped from a flat piece of timber.

Skirt See **Apron.**

Slip-in seat See **Drop-in seat.**

Sofa table A rectangular table with two hinged flaps at the ends, designed to stand behind a sofa.

Spade foot A tapering foot of square section.

Spandrel A decorative corner bracket, usually pierced and found at the tops of legs.

Splat The central upright in a chair back; loosely applied to all members in a chair back.

Squab The loose flat cushion on the seat of a chair.

Stiff-leaf toe cap A caster moulded with formalized leaves.

Stiles The vertical parts of a framework, a term usually associated with early furniture.

Stretchers The horizontal bars that unite and strengthen the legs of chairs and other furniture.

Stringing Fine inlaid lines around a piece of furniture.

Stuff-over seat A chair that is upholstered over the **seat rails.**

Swan-neck cresting A type of broken pediment with two S-shaped curves.

Swan-neck handle A curved handle, popular in the 18thC.

Teapoy A small piece of furniture designed for holding tea leaves.

Tenons See **Pegged framework.**

Thumb moulding Decorative convex moulding.

Toilet mirror Another term for a small dressing mirror with a box base, usually fitted with two or three drawers.

Trefoil Shaped like a clover, with three lobes.

Tripod table A small table with a round top supported by a three-legged pillar.

Turned A solid member modelled by turning on a lathe.

Uprights The vertical sides of the back of a chair.

Urn table A small 18thC table designed to hold a silver kettle or water urn.

Veneer A thin slice of timber cut from the solid.

Wainscot chair An early **joined** chair with a panelled back, open arms and a wooden seat.

Whatnot A mobile stand with open shelves.

Wheel-back chair A chair with a circular back with radiating spokes, associated with the late 18thC.

Windsor chair A type of wooden chair with a spindle back.

Wing chair A fully upholstered chair with " wings" at the sides to keep out draughts.

SELECTED MAKERS

In England, few cabinet-makers before the 19thC marked their wares, although in France, from the 18thC, it was quite common practice for the top *ébénistes* to stamp their wares, usually in the form of initials. Until very recently little attention had been paid to researching lesser known 19thC cabinet-makers but interest is now growing in marks and makers stamps or labels. In the United States, top cabinet-makers tended to leave documentary evidence of their products.

Adam, Robert 1728-1792
Scottish architect and furniture designer responsible for the revival of Neo-classicism in the 18thC. Worked mainly in mahogany and satinwood.

Affleck, Thomas 1740-95
Scottish-born cabinet-maker living in Philadelphia. Worked mainly in the Chinese Chippendale style.

Belter, John Henry 1804-1863
German-born exponent of the rococo style, working in the United States.

Boulle, André-Charles 1642-1732
Chief cabinet-maker to Louis XIV of France who gave his name to an elaborate marquetry technique using brass and tortoiseshell.

Bullock, George d.1818
British cabinet-maker particularly noted for his use of British woods and marbles.

Chippendale, Thomas 1718-1789
Son of a Worcestershire carver, Chippendale set up as a cabinet-maker in London in 1749. An exponent of the rococo style, his superb and delicate carving set new standards for furniture making. His *Gentleman and Cabinet Makers Director*, the first book of its kind, was published in 1754.

Chippendale, Thomas, the younger
Designer in his own right who continued his father's business in St. Martin's Lane.

Cobb, John d. 1778
Influential English cabinet-maker in partnership with John Vile.

Eastlake, Charles Locke 1836-1906
Designer and exponent of the "modern gothic" or "early English" style, the essential simplicity of which was described in his *Hints on Household Taste*, 184

published in 1868 and read widely both in England and the United States. No pieces made to his designs have ever been found.

Elfe, Thomas 1719-1795
English-born cabinet-maker who settled in Charleston, South Carolina, producing furniture in the Chippendale style with distinctive fretwork.

Gillows, estabd 1695
Furniture manufacturers founded in Lancaster, England. Moved to London in 1761 where they continued to produce well-made pieces. Merged with Warings in 1900.

Gibbons, Grinling 1648-1721
A remarkably gifted naturalistic carver. He was appointed master carver to George I in 1714.

Gimson, Ernest 1864-1919
Originally trained as an architect. Much impressed with Morris and the Arts and Crafts Movement, he became apprenticed to a chair-maker; thereafter he practised as a chair- and cabinet-maker in Gloucestershire.

Goddard, John 1723-85
Cabinet-maker working in Newport with Joe Townsend (see **Townsend-Goddard**). Partly responsible for the development of the Newport blockfront-and-shell style.

Hepplewhite, George d. 1786
English cabinet-maker of whom little is known and none of whose pieces survive – yet his name is synonymous with the post-Chippendale period. In 1788, a collection of some 300 designs "from drawings by A. Hepplewhite & Co., Cabinet-Makers" was published entitled *The Cabinet Maker's and Upholsterer's Guide*. It is upon the distinctively light and delicate styles shown in this book that his reputation rests.

Holland, Henry 1745-1806
Architect who favoured Anglo-French taste.

Hope, Thomas 1770-1831
English collector and designer favouring Neo-Greek and Egyptian styles.

Ince, William 1759-1803 and Mayhew, John d.1811
Reputable English partnership of cabinet-makers and upholsterers. Married two sisters on the same day (20th February, 1762). Their other joint effort, *The Universal System of Household Furniture*, a book of over 300 designs, rivalled Chippendale's *Director*.

Jacob, Georges 1739-1814
Leading French *ébéniste* of the
pre-Revolution years, working in
the Neo-classical style.
**Jacob-Desmalter, François
Honoré 1770-1841**
Son of Georges Jacob and a
leading cabinet-maker of the
French Empire style. Notable for
his use of bronze, mother-of-pearl
and porcelain decoration.
Jennens & Bettridge
Best known of the 19thC
producers of papier mâché
furniture. Wares are stamped.
Jones, Inigo 1573-1652
Well-known architect and
furniture designer of the English
Renaissance.
Kent, William 1685-1748
English architect, furniture
designer and landscape gardener
in the classical style.
**Le Gaigneur, Louis Constantin
active c.1815**
Boulle artist and cabinet-maker.
**Lock, Matthias, dates
unknown; active c.1740-c1765**
Carver and designer; pioneer of
the rococo style in England who
worked with Chippendale on the
Director (1754).
McLean, John active c. 1774
Cabinet-maker in the French
taste specializing in "Elegant
Parisian Furniture".
**Martin Brothers active mid
18thC**
French furniture makers
responsible for the development
of *vernis Martin*, a substitute for
Oriental laquer.
**Morel, Nicholas and Hughes,
Robert active c. 1795**
Cabinet-makers and upholsterers
to the Prince of Wales; much
influenced by French design.
Morris, William 1834-1896
Designer, artist-craftsman, poet,
and author, this multi-talented
"Apostle" of the Arts and Crafts
Movement advocated a return to
simple hand-crafted furniture.
Oakley, George active c.1782
Cabinet-maker to the Prince of
Wales.
Phyfe, Duncan 1768-1854
Renowned American maker; born
in Scotland, he settled in New
York where he produced designs
based on the English Regency
and French Empire styles.
**Pugin, Auguste Welby 1812-
1852**
English architect of French
descent and leading force behind
the 19thC Gothic revival in
England.
Riesenburgh, Bernard van

d.1767
French cabinet-maker responsible
for some of the finest examples of
rococo furniture of the Louis XV
period.
**Riesener, Jean-Henri 1734-
1806**
Master *ébéniste* to Louis XVI of
France producing rich and ornate
furniture.
Savery, William active 1740-87
Philadelphia-based cabinet-maker
renowned for his work in the
Queen Anne style during the
Chippendale period.
**Schinkel, Karl Friedrich 1727-
1801**
German architect and interior
designer who greatly influenced
the Biedermeier style of 19thC
Germany with simplicity and
comfort taking precedence over
decoration.
Seddon, George 1727-1801
Leading London cabinet-maker
of the late 18thC and founder of
Seddon & Co., a highly successful
workshop.
Shearer, Thomas end 18thC
Author of *The Cabinetmaker's
London Book of Prices* (1788), a
volume comparable to A
Hepplewhite's *Guide*.
Sheraton, Thomas 1751-1806
English designer and author of
several influential volumes on
furniture design. Best known for
light pieces, mainly in satinwood,
with restrained inlay.
Smith, George active until 1836
Cabinet-maker, upholsterer and
designer in the Regency style.
**Tatham, Charles Heathcote
1772-1842**
Joined **Henry Holland** in 1789,
when he was sent to Rome to
research Italian design. His
experiences, about which he
wrote several books, had a large
influence on furniture designs of
the period.
Taylor, John active c. 1824-9
English cabinet-maker who
worked with George Oakley
before setting up his own
business.
Townsend-Goddard
Renowned American partnership
of the American Chippendale
period. Job Townsend (1699-
1765) and his nephew, John
Townsend were the most
prominent members of the family,
which developed blockfront-and-
shell furniture.
Vile, William d. 1767
A leading English cabinet-maker
of the 18thC, in partnership with
Cobb.

BIBLIOGRAPHY

Agius, Pauline and Stephen Jones, *Ackermann's Regency Furniture and Interiors* (1984)

Airs, Malcolm, *The Making of the English Country House, 1500-1640* (1975)

Beck, D., *Book of American Furniture*

Bly, John, *Discovering English Furniture* (1976)
Is It Genuine? (1986)

Cescinsky, Herbert, *The Gentle Art of Faking Furniture* (1931)

Cescinsky, Herbert, and Ernest Gribble, *Early English Furniture and Woodwork* (1922)

Chinnery, Victor, *Oak Furniture – The British Tradition* (1979)

Coleridge, A., *Chippendale Furniture* (1968)

Collard, Frances, *Regency Furniture* (1983)

Comstock, Helen, *American Furniture: 17th, 18th and 19th century styles* (1962)
Victorian Furniture and Windsor Chairs (1958)

Edwards, Ralph, *Shorter Dictionary of English Furniture* (1964)
V&A Museum: Catalogue of English Furniture and Woodwork (1931)

Edwards, Ralph, and Margaret Jourdain, *Georgian Cabinet-Makers* (1955)

Fales, Dean A. Jr., *American Painted Furniture 1660-1680* (1973)

Fastnedge, Ralph, *Sheraton Furniture* (1983)

Gilbert, C., *Furniture at Temple Newsam House and Lotherton Hall* (1978)

Goodison, N., *Ormolu: The Work of Matthew Boulton* (1974)

Hayward, C.H., *English Period Furniture* (1984)

Hayward, Helena (ed.), *World Furniture* (1965)

Heal, Sir Ambrose, *The London Furniture Makers, 1660-1840* (1953)

Heckscher, Morrison, *American Furniture in the Metropolitan Museum of Art* (1972)

Hughes, Therle, *English Domestic Needlework* (1961)

Jackson-Stops, G., and J. Pipkin, *English Country House – A Grand Tour* (1985)

Jourdain, Margaret, *Regency Furniture* (1965)
English Decoration and Furniture of the Early Renaissance 1500-1650 (1924)
English Interior Decoration 1500-1830 (1950)

Jourdain, Margaret, and J. Rose, 186

English Furniture and the Georgian Period (1953)

Joy, Edward T., *English Furniture 1800-1851* (1977)

Kirk, John, *American Chairs, Queen Anne and Chippendale* (1972)

Macquoid, Percy, *A History of English Furniture* 4 vols (1919)
English Furniture, Tapestry and Needlework of the XVIth-XIXth Centuries

Miller, Judith and Martin, *Antiques Directory: Furniture* (1985)
Miller's Antiques Price Guide 1980-1991
Miller's Pocket Antiques Fact File (1988)
Miller's Pocket Dictionary of Antiques (1990)
Miller's Understanding Antiques (1989)

Montgomery, Charles F., *American Furniture, The Federal Period* (1966)

Moses, Michael, *Master Craftsmen of Newport* (1984)

Musgrave, Clifford, *Regency Furniture* (1961)
Adam and Hepplewhite and other Neo-Classical Furniture (1966)
Pictorial Dictionary of British 18th century Furniture Design (1976)

Nutting, Wallace, *Furniture Treasury, Vols. 1,2,3* (1928)

Payne, C., *Price Guide to 19th century European Furniture* (1985)

Pinto, Edward H., *Treen and other Wooden Bygones* (1969)

Sack, Albert, *Fine Points of Furniture* (1950)

Savage, G., *Dictionary of Antiques*

Sotheby's *Concise Encyclopedia of Furniture* (ed C. Payne) (1989)

Stevens-Claxton, Christopher, and Stewart Whittington, *18th century English Furniture: The Norman Adams Collection* (1983)

Stoneman, Vernon C., *John and Thomas Seymour* (1959)

Symonds, R.W., *English Furniture from Charles II to George II* (1929)
Furniture History Society (1965)

Symonds, W.R., and B.B. Whinneray, *Victorian Furniture* (1987)

Thornton, Peter, *Seventeenth Century Interior Decoration in England, France and Holland* (1978)

Ward-Jackson, Peter, *English Furniture Designs of the 18th century* (1984)

Wills, Geoffrey, *English Furniture 1550-1760* (1971)

Wolsey, S.W., and R.W.P. Luff, *Furniture in England – The Age of the Joiner* (1968)

INDEX

PICTURE CREDITS AND ACKNOWLEDGMENTS

The publishers would like to thank the following auction houses, museums, dealers, collectors and other sources for kindly supplying pictures for use in this book or for allowing their pieces to be photographed.

20 Wak; 21tr Wak, 21c & br PC; 22 HA; 23 HA; 24 MB; 25 MB; 28 WB; 29 l(x2) WB, 29r(x2) MB; 20 Hock; 31 Hock; 32 SL; 33(x3) MB; 34 CL; 35l CL, 35br SL; 36 Mill; 37l Mill, 37 r(x2) WB; 38 RD; 39(x3) RD; 40 WB; 41l(x2) WB, 41r CL; 42 JGM; 43l(x3), rt, rc JGM, 43br Griff; 44 RC; 45l(x3), rt, rc RC; 45br S; 46 WB; 47l(x2), tr WB, 47br SL; 50 Wak; 51(x2) RD; 52 HA; 53(x6) HA; 54 RD; 55 (x4) RD; 56 HA; 57(x2) HA; 58 Hum; 59l Hum; 59r(x2) SNY; 60 WB; 61l(x2), rt, rb WB; 62 PJ; 63(x4) PJ; 64 WB; 65(x2) WB; 66 Hock; 67l(x2) Hock, 67r SL; 74 RD; 75l(x3) RD, 75r(2) Ren; 76 JGM; 77l(x2) JGM, 77r(x2) WB; 78 RC; 79tl RC, 79bl SL, 79r(x2) SL; 80 LB; 81l(x2) LB, 81rt, rc LB, 81br SL; 82 CL; 83(x2) CL; 84 Ren; 85(x2) Ren; 86 WB; 87l(x3) WB; 87rt WB, 87 rb SNY; 90 MB; 91(x3) MB; 92(x2) WB; 93(x5) WB; 94 Wak; 95l(x2) Wak, 95r SL; 96 JGM; 97l(x2), rt JGM, 97br Hock; 98 Mill; 99(x4) Mill; 100 RD; 101(x3) RD; 102 Wak; 103l(x3) Wak, 103r CL; 104 WB; 105(x2) WB; 106 WB; 107l(x3) WB, 107r SL; 108 LB; 109(x2) LB; 116 MB; 117lCL, 117r SL; 118 RD; 119(x3) RD; 120 HA; 121(x4) HA; 122 Hum; 123(x2) Hum; 124 WB; 125l(x2), tr WB, 125br CNY; 126 SL; 127 SL; 128 PJ; 129tl, tr PJ, 129br Phil; 130 JGM; 131(x2) JGM; 132 WB; 133 SL; 134 WB; 135(x2) WB; 136 Wil; 137l, tr Wil, 137br SNY; 138 Hock; 139l(x2) Hock, 139tr CL, 139br SL; 142 RD; 143(x3) RD; 144 WB; 145(x5) WB; 146 JGM; 147 JGM; 148 WB; 149(x3) WB; 150 JGM; 151(x3) PJ; 152 LB; 153(x3) LB; 154 WB; 155(x2) WB; 160 WB; 161 WB; 162 SL; 163 SL; 164 Ren; 165l (x3), tr Ren, 165br WB; 166 RC; 167l(x2) RC, 167r SL; 168 LB; 169(x3) LB; 170 SL; 171l CL, 171tr SL, 171br CL; 172 SL; 173l SL; 173r CL; 174 SL; 175 CL; 176 WB; 177 CL; 178 CL; 179(x2) CL

KEY
b bottom, c centre, l left r right, t top

CL	Christie's, London	Phil	Philip Cooper Antiques, Petworth, West Sussex
Griff	Griffin Antiques, Petworth, West Sussex	PJ	Patrick Jefferson Antiques, London
HA	Huntington Antiques Ltd, Stow-on-the-Wold Gloucerstershire	RC	Rupert Cavendish Antiques, London
		RD	Richard Davidson Antiques, Arundel, West Sussex
Hock	William Hockley Antiques, Petworth, West Sussex		
Hum	Humphry Antiques, Petworth, West Sussex	Ren	Rendall Antiques, London
JGM	John G. Morris Ltd, Petworth, West Sussex	SL	Sotheby's London
		SNY	Sotheby's New York
LB	Lesley Bragge Antiques, Petworth, West Sussex	Wak	Michael Wakelin and Helen Linfield, Petworth, West Sussex
MB	Mitchell Beazley International	WB	William Bedford PLC, London
Mill	Millhouse Antiques, Petworth, West Sussex	Wil	T. G. Wilkinson Antiques, Petworth, West Sussex
PC	Private Collection		

Thanks are also due to Deirdre Davidson and Heritage Restorations of Petworth, West Sussex for their help in the preparation of this book.

Special photography by Ian Booth and Nigel O'Gorman